ELITEAVIATIONS

M000311644

AIRLINE TRANSPORT
PILOT PRACTICAL TEST STANDARDS
EXPLAINED FOR ELITE PERFORMANCE

AN EXTENSIVE GUIDE TO HELP PILOTS FULLY
UNDERSTAND THE REQUIREMENTS OF THE AIRLINE
TRANSPORT PILOT AND AIRCRAFT TYPE RATING
PRACTICAL TEST STANDARDS

BY **ELITE AVIATION SOLUTIONS**

The purpose of this book is to assist pilots in preparing for the ATP Practical Test. The user of this information assumxes all risk and liability arising from such use. The ATP Practical Test and information provided by the FAA are the final authority. The additional information provided is to assist in understanding the practical test and the techniques can be used by the pilot at their own risk.

While every attempt is made to ensure that the information in this manual is correct, no liability can be accepted by the author or publisher for loss, damage or injury caused by any errors in, or omissions from, the information given.

TABLE OF CONTENTS

PREFACE

Most pilots do not fully understand what is expected of them during the practical test. Most pilots do not review the ATP Practical Test Standards (PTS) completely prior to their practical test. I believe most pilots take a practical test for a pilot certificate with very little understanding of what is expected of them.

Would any professional reaching the highest rating in any profession take a major exam without extensively preparing for the exam? By far most would not. Believe it or not this happens often with the ATP pilot certificate.

When I ask pilots preparing for their Airline Transport Pilot rating if they have reviewed the ATP PTS, most indicate they briefly reviewed it or not at all. Most pilots I have worked with have not extensively reviewed all of the resources referenced in the PTS. All of these resources are fair game on the practical test. Most pilots are taking their ATP practical test with very little preparation.

During initial training for a specific aircraft in many training centers pilots often obtain a type rating and sometimes their ATP certificate. In the two weeks of training pilots are overwhelmed with an immense amount of information about an aircraft they have never flown, and at the end of this training the pilot takes a practical test. I have asked a few pilots attending initial training for an ATP and type certificate if they had reviewed the ATP PTS. The pilots answered "no" almost every time. The others barely reviewed the PTS. At this point it's a little late to fully understand what is required of the pilot on the practical test. These pilots did not have enough time because the training in the next two weeks was going to occupy all of their time.

By far the majority of pilots take a practical test understanding very little of what is expected of them and the structure of the practical test. Most pilots do receive their ATP certificate, but there are some that fail to pass due to a lack of understanding. There are some pilots that fail, I think unjustly because the examiner does not fully understand the PTS and the pilot does not either.

Some pilots may say, if I just follow the guidance of the examiner and do what he asks I really don't need to understand all the details of the practical test. In all reality this is how most practical tests are conducted, the applicant is somewhat prepared for the practical test by the instructor and the pilot is told what to expect. This is a fairly canned practical test with little aeronautical decision making. He just does what the examiner asks and at the end, the pilot receives their pilot certificate most of the time.

A problem is that some pilots have failed their practical test because of an incorrect interpretation by the examiner. The examiner thought they were right, but in the examples that I know of based on the practical test standards and other supporting FAA information, pilots have failed their practical test and should not have failed. If the pilot had a good working knowledge of the practical test standards and some of the other FAA information, the pilot could have challenged the examiner's decision.

This book contains the majority of the ATP PTS with additional information. I attempted keep it simple and to the point because your time valuable. I excluded some sections like those related to seaplanes to reduce the reading time. The understanding a pilot develops from the other sections can easily be applied to the seaplane sections. I hope with the additional information your knowledge of each required area of operation and task will increase and you will be much better prepared for your ATP practical test.

I will reference at times additional information located in other FAA guidance. If you would like to be fully prepared for your practical test I would advise obtaining a copy of those guides.

"Success depends upon previous
preparation, and without such preparation
there is sure to be failure."
–CONFUCIUS

Layout of the Book

Objective and element are used interchangeably.

Sections of the ATP PTS that help explain points and information are included in this book. The layout of this book follows the ATP PTS format which will allow a pilot to easily correlate the information with the ATP PTS.

The current ATP PTS is what controls a pilot's practical test. Use it with this book to fully understand what is expected.

This Book is Based on the Current ATP PTS

AIRLINE TRANSPORT PILOT AND AIRCRAFT TYPE RATING

Practical Test Standards For AIRPLANE

July 2008

FAA-S-8081-5F with Changes 1, 2, 3 &4

Note: the goal of this book is to help pilots understand the PTS and help pilots be fully prepared for the practical test. Some information located in the ATP PTS that does not meet this goal is omitted. This book is not meant to replace the ATP PTS. This book is to supplement your study material for the ATP PTS. Your time is valuable and I want the information to be as simple as possible. Information and tasks related to seaplanes are omitted. Please refer to the PTS for the related tasks.

Please reference the current ATP PTS located at www.FAA.gov for the most current and up-to-date information.

FOREWORD

The Airline Transport Pilot and Aircraft Type Rating—Airplane Practical Test Standards (PTS) book has been published by the Federal Aviation Administration (FAA) to establish the standards for **airline transport pilot and aircraft type rating practical tests for airplanes. FAA inspectors, designated pilot examiners, and check airmen (referred to as examiners throughout the remaining practical test standard) must conduct practical tests in compliance with these standards. Flight instructors and applicants should find these standards helpful in practical test preparation.** 3

The FAA has indicated that examiners must conduct practical tests in compliance with these standards. The FAA also indicates that flight instructors and applicants should find these standards helpful in preparation for the test. The problem is most applicants have minimal knowledge about the ATP PTS.

INTRODUCTION

General Information

The Flight Standards Service of the Federal Aviation Administration (FAA) has developed the practical test standard (PTS) to be used by examiners when conducting airline transport pilot and aircraft type rating practical tests in airplanes. **Instructors are expected to address all of the elements contained in this PTS when preparing applicants for practical tests.** Applicants should be familiar with this PTS and refer to these standards during their training. 3

Plan Ahead

Instructors are expected to address **all of the objectives (elements)** in the PTS and applicants should be familiar with the associated PTS. If a pilot does not hear the instructor referencing the ATP PTS throughout training that pilot should be concerned. The FAA would like pilots to be familiar with the ATP PTS and being familiar the PTS cannot happen in just a few hours. Pilots really need to prepare ahead of time. Between the PTS and other sources of guidance by the FAA it is a very confusing maze of information. Even though the FAA makes it sound like the PTS is all, there is so much other guidance examiners use.

Here is an example I know of where the instructor was not training using the Instrument Rating PTS and the student was not familiar with the Instrument Rating PTS. The pilot was cleared to an NDB but began tracking to the incorrect station because the station was not properly tuned and identified. Identifying the station is required in the PTS under that task. The instructor did not emphasize this during training and the pilot did not realize that this was a requirement during the practical test. This failure could of easily been avoided with proper training.

Instructors are human and some instructors are better than others. Too often pilots rely 100% on their instructors to guide them and this is a big mistake. Take control of your practical test preparation and work with your instructor to be the best prepared you can be. Some instructors will prepare you very well and some will not. Sometimes there is just not enough time or money for the instructor to fully prepare a pilot. To be 100% prepared the pilot must begin training with much of the practical test preparation complete. For example, all of the references and tasks reviewed for proper knowledge level.

In the above example, the instructor preparing that pilot may not have thought that identifying navigation stations was very important because it wasn't emphasized during training. Maybe the instructor didn't emphasize this because it wasn't emphasized to him by his instructor. In the end, this pilot failed the practical test because of not properly identifying the station and tracked to the wrong navigation station. The bottom line is identify the station is important for safety and it is required by the PTS under certain tasks. It was stated in the PTS and if the pilot and/or the instructor covered every element of the PTS as indicated by the FAA, the pilot would not of failed the practical test.

Take your time and prepare thoroughly. This will reduce your chances of failing your practical test and it will greatly reduce your stress. I think a main reason why pilots get so stressed out over practical tests is that they don't feel prepared and don't fully understand what is expected of them.

Understanding what is expected of you during your practical test will greatly reduce your stress. Understand every task and understand every objective of each task. That is the way to be fully prepared and fully understand what is expected of you.

Special note. If a pilot would like to have a career as a professional pilot, the new Airline Safety and FAA Extension Act of 2010 is enabling employers to track a pilots training record much better. It has always been important to avoid practical test failures in the past but it is even more important now. Strive for a perfect training record! Don't fail a practical test because you didn't understand what is required.

Higher Level

Preparing for your ATP practical test is an opportunity for a pilot to be average or be better than most other pilots. Take this opportunity to increase you knowledge and professionalism. So many pilots have passed their ATP practical test and didn't know much of the information required by the ATP PTS. Is this a failure of the system? Don't slip by because the system doesn't require pilots to demonstrate knowledge and skills needed to obtain the highest pilot rating. Preparing thoroughly for the ATP practical test will pay dividends for years to come and may even save your life and others someday. Professional pilots need to know an immense amount of information and unlike a lot of professions, that knowledge can save lives, even yours.

This is your opportunity to learn and excel!

"Education is not preparation for life; education is life itself."

–JOHN DEWEY

Practical Test Standard Concept

Title 14 of the Code of Federal Regulations (14 CFR) part 61 specifies the areas in which knowledge and skill must be demonstrated by the applicant before the issuance of an airline transport pilot certificate and/ or a type rating in airplanes. The CFRs provide the flexibility to permit the FAA to publish practical test standards containing the AREAS OF OPERATION and specific TASKs in which pilot competency must be demonstrated. Title 49 of the U.S. Code (Transportation) requires the administrator to promulgate rules and set standards in the interest of public safety. [3]

Adherence to provisions of the regulations and the PTS is mandatory for the evaluation of airline transport pilot and type rating applicants. For some aircraft types, however, provisions of FAA Flight Standardization Board (FSB) Reports may specify special details as to how 14 CFR part 61 and this PTS apply to certain maneuvers, TASKs, procedures, or knowledge areas. FSB Reports are available from the Flight Standards Service System Safety's web site at: http://fsims.faa. gov. [3]

What You Need to Know About FSB Reports

Visit the following link to research an aircraft for a FSB report. If your aircraft does not have a FSB report, then you don't need to read this section. If you are interested in understanding what a FSB report is then continue reading.

http://fsims.faa.gov/PICResults.aspx?mode=Publication&doctype=FSB%20Reports

Thousands of pilots have taken practical tests not fully understanding what FSB reports are and how they apply to certain aircraft and to the PTS. FSB is referenced in many tasks and many pilots don't know what it is. I would also estimate that many instructors have prepared pilots for practical tests and did not explain this part of the PTS to them. Granted many pilots will take practical tests in aircraft that are not affected by a FSB report. Pilots should still understand what a FSB report is because someday they may use one on a practical test that has a report.

Time Saver!

1. Check FSB link for your aircraft.

2. No FSB report, skip to next section. FSB report –

3. Continue reading to understand the report.

4. Read the FSB report on the aircraft.

FAA 8900.1 Establishment of a FSB

An aircraft evaluation group (AEG) decides when to establish a FSB. FSBs are usually established for large turbojet and turbo propeller aircraft, Special Federal Aviation Regulation (SFAR) 41 airplanes, and Title 14 of the Code of Federal Regulations (14 CFR) part 23 commuter category airplanes. FSBs are not usually established for 14 CFR part 23 and 27 aircraft, unless the aircraft have unique design, flight, or handling characteristics. 4

Responsibilities of the FSB

The FSBs primary responsibilities are to determine the requirements for pilot type ratings, to develop minimum training recommendations, and to ensure initial flight crewmember competency in accordance with Advisory Circular (AC) 120-53, Crew Qualification and Pilot

Type Rating Requirements for Transport Category Aircraft Operated Under 14 CFR Part 121. This information is published in a report that is sent to AFS-200 for coordination. After approval, it is to be used by the principal operations inspector (POI) as guidance in approving operator training, checking, and currency programs. The report is distributed to field offices through the master minimum equipment list (MMEL) subsystem of the Aviation Safety Analysis System (ASAS) data base. Specific functions of the FSB are as follows:

A. Determination of Pilot Type Ratings. The FSB determines the requirement for a pilot type rating for new aircraft usually during certification flight tests. The FSB also evaluates differences in follow-on aircraft to determine if a new pilot type rating is required.

B. Development of Training Objectives. The FSB develops training objectives for normal and emergency procedures and maneuvers and reviews training device requirements.

C. Training Recommendations. The FSB publishes recommendations for use by POIs during approval of an operator's training program. In developing training objectives and procedures, the FSB considers unique requirements of an aircraft such as the fly-by-wire electronic flight control system and the side-stick controller of the Airbus 320.

D. Initial Training/Checking. Board members usually conduct initial training and checking of the manufacturer's pilots and FAA operations inspectors.

E. Review of Existing Training Programs. When required, the FSB may review training programs for existing aircraft to evaluate the effectiveness of the training.

F. Accidents. In case of an accident, FSB members may be consulted on training or crewmember competency issues involving aircraft assigned to the board. [4]

FSB Report

After concurrence by AFS-200, the FSB report is approved by the AEG office manager. FSB reports are entered into the ASAS data base where they are available to FAA field offices. The FSB report should contain the recommended minimum training requirements that operations inspectors may use when evaluating operator training programs.

A. Report Considerations. FSB reports are based on a variety of factors, including private sector comments, flight test evaluation, and operating experience.

B. Final Determinations and Findings. The FSB may hold public meetings and invite private sector groups to attend, after which the FSB will make a final determination and issue recommendations.

C. Contents of the FSB Report. The FSB report should contain the following:

- The assignment of type ratings

- A recommendation of minimum training, checking, and currency requirements

- Any special training requirements

NOTE: The FSB report contains only **recommended** minimum training requirements. Further guidance on training program approval is found in AC 120-53 and in volume 3 of 8900.1. 4

Time Saver!

In preparing for the ATP practical test most pilots will not have a need to view AC 120-53. The above is a general description of a FSB report. Checking your aircraft for a FSB report is probably all the time you need to spend on FSB Reports

Example:

The Challenger 604 (CL-604) has a FSB report. Under checking the following is provided:

The following areas of emphasis must be demonstrated during checking:

a. Proficiency in manual and automatic (including FMS and auto throttle) flight in normal, abnormal, and emergency situations must be demonstrated at each proficiency/competency check by all crewmembers.

b. The use of manual modes to operate systems such as electrical, hydraulic, pressurization, flight controls, etc. and emergency equipment, such as the ADG, must be demonstrated at each proficiency/competency check by all crewmembers.

c. Demonstration of a no flap approach and landing during a pilot type rating or 14 CFR part 135 check is required per the Airline Transport Pilot and/ or Type Rating Practical Test Standards - FAA-S-8081 Area of Operation VI, Task F. In accordance with Order 8400.10, Volume 5, Chapter 2 when the flight demonstration is conducted in an airplane, verses a simulator, touchdown from a no flap approach is not required. The approach should be flown to the point where the inspector or examiner can deter-mine whether a touchdown at an acceptable point on the runway and a safe landing to a full-stop could be made.

Note: 8400.10 has been incorporated into 8900.10.

FSB reports also provide differences between similar aircraft for example the CL-604 and the CL-605. These differences are categorized by a training level which are A, B, C, D. The levels are provided in AC 120-53A.

Again using the CL-604 and CL-605 aircraft FSB report, it also identifies training program special emphasis items. The FSB has identified several aircraft systems and/or procedures (listed below) that should receive special emphasis in an approved CL-604 Training Program, or CL-605 Training Program where applicable:

Flight Training (Full Flight Simulator - Level C or D and/or aircraft):

a. Dual hydraulic system malfunctions (system 1 or 2, and system 3)

b. Air Driven Generator (ADG) deployment

c. ILS approach on standby instruments

d. Primary Flight Display (PFD), Multifunction Display (MFD), EICAS status page reversionary modes

e. Inability to exclusively use EICAS messages to determine aircraft system status. Some switches (i.e. L/R to aux fuel transfer, fuel crossflow, and AC essential bus transfer) are not represented by EICAS messages.

A no flap landing in CL-604 or CL-605 is a training program special emphasis item.

Special emphasis during training should be placed in the area of roll control during multiple hydraulic system failure, crosswind landing and rollout, and zero-flap landing.

The FSB has determined that zero-flap approaches and landings to a full stop are required to be demonstrated by applicants seeking type certification in this aircraft. The aircraft's trailing edge flap extension is powered by the electrical system and there is no alternate means of flap operation in the case of electrical system failure. The aircraft has a relatively high approach and landing speed and has a tendency to "float" if normal landing flare technique is used. Thrust reverser deployment during a zero flap landing tends to cause the nose to pitch-up, requiring significant pilot input to maintain nose wheel contact with the runway.

After the brief discussion above with examples you get the idea of how a FSB report can affect the training and checking in certain aircraft. Be prepared and visit the FAA FSB report website and research your particular aircraft.

Visit the following link to research your aircraft for a FSB report.

http://fsims.faa.gov/PICResults.aspx?mode=Publication&doctype=FSB%20Reports

Note: Pilots employed by an air carrier certificate holder, operating under 14 CFR part 121 or 135, or as authorized by the Administrator, whose manual prohibits a circling approach when the weather is below 1,000 feet and 3 miles' visibility, are not required to be checked on the circling approach and landing from a circling approach. Aircraft type

ratings added to an airline transport pilot certificate issued without training and checking in the circling maneuver, as authorized, will be annotated "MD-11 CIRC. APCH-VMC ONLY," for example. This restriction may be removed when the circling approach is satisfactorily demonstrated to a designated examiner, a check airman who is a designated examiner, or an FAA inspector, in the appropriate type airplane. If, under 14 CFR part 121 or 135, or as authorized by the Administrator, the initial airline transport pilot certificate is issued coincident with a type rating, with a circling approach restriction, the airline transport pilot certificate will be annotated, "ATP CIRC. APCHVMC ONLY, MD-11 CIRC. APCH-VMC ONLY," for example. This restriction to the airline transport pilot certificate level will be removed when the first unrestricted airline transport pilot certificate or airline transport pilot type rating is issued. The respective circling approach restriction will then be annotated on the certificate, as listed in the first example. 3

Practical Test Book Description

This practical test book contains the Airline Transport Pilot and Aircraft Type Rating Practical Test Standards - Airplane. The Airline Transport Pilot and Aircraft Type Rating Practical Test Standards - Airplane includes AREAS OF OPERATION and TASKs for the initial issuance of an airline transport pilot certificate and for the addition of category, class, and aircraft type ratings to an airline transport pilot certificate. These AREAS OF OPERATION and TASKs also apply for the issuance of an airplane type rating to a private or commercial pilot certificate.

The AREAS OF OPERATION are divided into two sections. The first AREA OF OPERATION in each section is conducted on the ground to determine the applicant's knowledge of the aircraft, equipment, performance, and limitations.

The eight AREAS OF OPERATION located in the second section, numbered II-IX, are considered to be the flight portion of the practical test. All eight of these AREAS OF OPERATION test the applicant's knowledge and skills.

If **all TASKs** of the practical test are not completed on one date, all remaining TASKs of the test must be satisfactorily completed not more than 60 calendar days after the date on which the applicant began the test. 3

Very important!

The above information states that all tasks are required to be completed. To complete a task, all applicable objectives must be completed. No tasks can be omitted by the examiner. This point is missed by examiners and pilots a lot. The one exception is in 8900.1 where there is an exception for 121/135 operators. I have not read anywhere that an examiner examining an ATP Practical Test under part 91 can omit any task.

The ATP PTS is the only PTS that indicates a division between the ground and flight portions of the practical test. Many pilots misinterpret this as the examiner can not ask questions during the flight portion. That is partly right, the examiner cannot continue the equipment examination into the flight portion. But if during the flight portion the pilot doesn't demonstrate adequate knowledge during a task the examiner can at the appropriate time question the pilot to ensure adequate knowledge for that task.

AREAS OF OPERATION are phases of the practical test arranged in a logical sequence within each standard. They begin with Preflight Preparation and end with Post flight Procedures. The examiner may combine TASKs with similar objectives and conduct the practical test in any sequence that will result in a complete and efficient test; however, **the ground portion of the practical test must be accomplished before the flight portion**. TASKs are titles of knowledge areas, flight procedures, or maneuvers appropriate to an AREA OF OPERATION. 3

REFERENCES identify the publication(s) that describe(s) the TASK. Descriptions of specific TASKs are not included in the practical test standards because this information can be found in the current issue of the listed references. Publications other than those listed may be used for references if their content conveys substantially the same meaning as the referenced publications. [3]

Plan Ahead

Plan ahead and try to at least browse all the listed references. Some of the references you may have read from previous training but many of them you have not.

Indicated above is that other references can be used as long as the content conveys substantially the same meaning as the referenced publications. I personally would interpret this statement as the examiner should not ask a question from a non-listed reference where the answer to that question is not provided in the listed references in the PTS under that task. References not listed under a particular task can be used to support the information in the references provided for each task.

Example: The examiner asks a system question where the answer can not be found in the systems section of the POH but can be found in a reference not listed under that task. This is not a valid question. If the answer to that systems question can be found in the POH, then the other reference can be used to support that answer.

If a limit was not put on the references, an examiner could ask questions from the maintenance manual for example, and most applicants do not have access to this manual. Another example, it is not fair for an examiner to ask a question from a magazine article the pilot has never read. The best approach for the examiner is to ask questions where the answer is available in the listed references under that task.

There will be a few references below that lead to a dead end for that particular document but a pilot should be able to determine what document it was replaced by or incorporated into.

The ATP Practical Test Standard is Based on the Following References:

Public Law - 110-135 Dated 12-12-2007

14 CFR part 1 - Definitions and Abbreviations

14 CFR parts 23/25 - Airworthiness Standards

14 CFR part 61 - Certification: Pilots, Flight Instructors, and Ground Instructors

14 CFR part 71 - Designation of Class A, B, C, D, and E Airspace Areas; Airways; Air- Traffic Service; Routes; and Reporting points

14 CFR part 91 - General Operating and Flight Rules

14 CFR part 121 - Operating Requirements: Domestic, flag, and Supplemental Operations

14 CFR part 135 - Operating Requirements: Commuter and On Demand Operations and Rules Governing Persons on Board Such Aircraft

14 CFR part 139 - Certification and Operations

49 CFR part 830 - Notification and Reporting of Aircraft Accidents or Incidents and Overdue Aircraft, and Preservation of Aircraft Wreckage, Mail, Cargo, and Records

FAA-H-8083-1 - Aircraft Weight and Balance Handbook

FAA-H-8083-3 - Airplane Flying Handbook

FAA-H-8083-15 - Instrument Flying Handbook

FAA-H-8083-23 - Seaplane, Skiplane, and Float/Ski Equipped Helicopter Operations Book

FAA-H-8083-25 - Pilot's Handbook of Aeronautical Knowledge

FAA-H-8261-1 - Instrument Procedures Handbook

AC 00-2 - Advisory Circular Checklist

AC 00-6 - Aviation Weather

AC 00-45 - Aviation Weather Services

AC 20-29 - Use of Aircraft Fuel Anti-icing Additives

AC 20-117 - Hazards Following Ground Deicing and Ground Operations in Conditions Conducive to Aircraft Icing Aeronautical Decision Making

AC 60-22 - Aeronautical Decision Making

AC 60-28 - English Language Skill Standards Required by 14 CFR parts 61, 63, and 65

AC 61-84 - Role of Preflight Preparation

AC 61-134 - General Aviation Controlled flight into Terrain Awareness

AC 61-136 - FAA Approval of Basic Aviation Training Devices (BATD) and Advanced Aviation Training Devices (AATD)

AC 90-79 - Recommended Practices and Procedures for the Use of Long-Range Navigation

AC 90-91 - North American Route Program (NRP)

AC 90-94 - Guidelines for Using Global Positioning System Equipment for Non Precision Instrument Approaches in the U.S. National Airspace system

AC 90-100 - U.S. Terminal and En Route Area Navigation (RNAV) Operations

AC 91-43 - Unreliable Airspeed Indications

AC 91-51 - Effect of Icing on Aircraft Control and Airplane Deice and Anti-ice Systems

AC 91-70 - Oceanic Operations

AC 91-73 - Part 91 and Part 135 Single-Pilot Procedures During Taxi Operations

AC 91-74 - Pilot Guide - Flight in Icing Conditions

AC 91-79 - Runway Overrun Prevention

AC 120-27 - Aircraft Weight and Balance Control

AC 120-28 Criteria for Approval of Category III Landing Weather Minima for Takeoff, Landing, and Rollout

AC 120-29 - Criteria for Approval of Category I and Category II Weather Minima for Approach

AC 120-51 - Crew Resource Management Training

AC 120-57 - Surface Movement Guidance System

AC 120-60 - Ground Deicing and Anti-icing Program

AC 120-62 - Takeoff Safety Training Aid

AC 120-74 - Parts 91, 121, 125, and 135 Flight Crew Procedures During Taxi Operations

AC 135-17 - Pilot Guide Small Aircraft Ground Deicing

AC 150-5340-18 - Standards for Airport Sign Systems

AFD - Airport Facility Directory

AFM - FAA-Approved Airplane Flight Manual

AIM - Aeronautical Information Manual

CDL - Configuration Deviation List

DP - Departure Procedures

FDC NOTAM - National Flight Data Center Notices to Airmen

FSB Reports - Flight Standardization Board Reports

IAP - Instrument Approach Procedure

IFIM - International Flight Information Manual

MEL - Minimum Equipment List

NOTAM - Notices to Airmen

ODP - Obstacle Departure Procedure

Other - En Route Low and High Altitude Charts, Profile Descent Charts, Pertinent Pilot's Operating Handbooks, and Flight Manuals

SIAP - Standard Instrument Approach Procedure Charts

STAR - Standard Terminal Arrival

Note: The latest revision of these references should be used. 3

Objectives

Objectives list the important elements that must be satisfactorily performed to demonstrate competency in a TASK. Objectives include:

1. Specifically what the applicant should be able to do,

2. The conditions under which the TASK is to be performed, and

3. The acceptable standards of performance.

All TASKs are required, except as noted. The funny thing is there is no exceptions in the PTS as noted. When a particular element (objective) is not appropriate to the aircraft or its equipment, that element may be omitted. **A pilot should be prepared to know or demonstrate every element of every objective in the PTS that applies to the aircraft being used.** If a pilot is prepared with both the knowledge and the skills for every objective that applies to the pilot and aircraft, a pilot will do very well on the practical test. 3

Notice above the FAA states basically that the objectives include elements that must be satisfactorily performed to demonstrate competency in a TASK. I interpret this as saying that each element that is applicable must be satisfactorily performed and that no element of any objective can be omitted. Granted some elements will not apply to a particular aircraft and can't be demonstrated. The bottom line based on this information, the objective lists the elements that must be satisfactorily performed to complete the task. All applicable elements must be completed if the aircraft permits it. This is quite challenging to do in a practical test.

Every objective states at least, "To determine that the applicant." This objective is followed by the elements that need to be completed to meet that objective. Meeting the objectives satisfactorily completes that task. Meeting every objective in a practical test is difficult and requires a lot of organization on the examiners part. Many practical tests are conducted not completely meeting the objective of each task.

For example, the task Departure Procedures. The objective two-way communication failure is often not completed.

Located in the PTS is the examiners responsibility. There it is stated "the examiner who conducts the practical test is responsible for determining that the applicant meets the standards outlined in the Objective of each TASK within the AREAS OF OPERATION in the practical test standard. The examiner must meet this responsibility by determining that the applicant's knowledge and skill meet the Objective in all required TASKs."

I think this makes it clear what should be completed:

- Every task.

- Every objective.

- Every objective (element) that applies to the applicant and/or aircraft.

If a pilot finds themselves in a disagreement with the examiner about whether the pilot correctly met the requirements of a particular task the pilot should reread the above information on objectives. It says that each element must be satisfactorily performed to demonstrate competency in a task. The examiner must be able to specifically state that a pilot did not demonstrate a certain task appropriately. If a pilot can go down through the list of elements of a particular task and he successfully demonstrated each one, then the pilot should probably pass the task as long as the outcome was never seriously in doubt.

NOTES are used to emphasize special considerations required in the AREAS OF OPERATION or TASKs.

Abbreviations

14 CFR - Title 14 of the Code of Federal Regulations

AC - Advisory Circular

ADM - Aeronautical Decision Making

AGL - Above Ground Level

AMEL - Airplane Multiengine Land

AMES - Airplane Multiengine Sea

ATC - Air Traffic Control

CDL - Configuration Deviation List

CFIT - Controlled Flight into Terrain

CRM - Crew Resource Management

DA - Decision Altitude

DH - Decision Height

DP - Departure Procedure

FAA - Federal Aviation Administration

FAF - Final Approach Fix

FDC - Flight Data Center

FE - Flight Engineer

FMS - Flight Management System

FMSP - Flight Management System Procedures

FSB - Flight Standardization Board

FSD - Flight Simulation Device

FSDO - Flight Standards District Office

FTD - Flight Training Device

GLS - GNSS Landing System

GNSS - Global Navigation Satellite System

GPO - Government Printing Office

GPS - Global Positioning System

IAP - Instrument Approach Procedure

IFR - Instrument Flight Rules

ILS - Instrument Landing System

INS - Inertial Navigation System

LAHSO - Land and Hold Short Operations

LDA - Localizer-type Directional Aid

LOC - ILS Localizer

MDA - Minimum Descent Altitude

MEL - Minimum Equipment List

NAVAID - Navigation Aid

NDB - Non-directional Beacon

NOTAM - Notice to Airmen

NWS - National Weather Service

POH - Pilot's Operating Handbook

PT - Procedure Turn

PTS - Practical Test Standard

RNAV - Area Navigation

SRM - Single-Pilot Resource Management

STAR - Standard Terminal Arrival

TAA - Terminal Arrival Area

V1 - Takeoff Decision Speed

V2 - Takeoff Safety Speed

VDP - Visual Descent Point

VFR - Visual Flight Rules

VMC - Minimum Control Speed with Critical Engine Inoperative

VMC - Visual Meteorological Conditions

VOR - Very High Frequency Ominidirectional Range

VR - Rotation Speed

VREF - Reference Landing Approach Speed

VSSE - Safe, Intentional, One-Engine Inoperative Speed

VX - Best Angle of Climb Speed

VY - Best Rate of Climb Speed

Use of the Practical Test Standards

The TASKs in this PTS are for an initial airline transport pilot certificate, or the addition of a category, class, or aircraft type rating to an airline transport pilot certificate. All appropriate TASKs required for an initial type rating are also required for pilot-in-command proficiency checks conducted in accordance with 14 CFR part 61, section 61.58.

All TASKs are required, except as noted. When a particular element is not appropriate to the aircraft or its equipment, that element may be omitted. 3

The PTS indicates "when a particular element is not appropriate to the aircraft or its equipment, that element may be omitted." 3 For example under the emergency procedures task, the examiner can select certain emergencies. But under a particular task if it is not stated that the examiner has an option, then plan on demonstrating every element of that task if it applies to the aircraft used.

As stated above, "when a particular element is not appropriate to the aircraft or its equipment, that element may be omitted." This means every element is required except as noted or if it doesn't apply.

Example, under the task rejected takeoff, the elements indicate the rejected takeoff is due to an engine failure. I have seen practical tests where the rejected takeoff was due to a warning annunciator and not an engine failure. Technically according to the PTS the elements of the rejected takeoff were not completed, therefore the task was not completed.

An examiner is required to use the PTS to administer a practical test. The benefit to the person being evaluated is having a little bit of a heads up of what to expect. During a rejected takeoff it should be a simulated engine failure or in a simulator it will be an actual engine failure.

Example, under the departure procedures task objective 7 requires the pilot to exhibit adequate knowledge of two-way radio communications failure procedures. This is a heads up to review this information.

Objective 9 of the task departure procedures requires the pilot to accurately track a course, radial, or bearing. Element 10 requires the departure phase to be completed.

If the multiengine airplane used for the flight check does not publish a VMC, then the "Limited to Centerline Thrust" restriction will be added to any certificate issued from this check, unless competence in a multiengine airplane with a published VMC has already been demonstrated. 3

Examples of element exceptions are: integrated flight systems for aircraft not so equipped, operation of landing gear in fixed gear aircraft, multiengine TASKs in single-engine aircraft, or other situations where the aircraft operation is not compatible with the requirement of the element. 3 This statement from the PTS validates even more that all objectives (elements) are included unless there is an exception or the aircraft is not equipped to do the element. 3 There are not many exceptions throughout the PTS.

If an applicant refuses to demonstrate a requested maneuver, the examiner may issue a Letter of Discontinuance to allow the examiner and applicant to discuss the applicant's concern about the requested maneuver, or a Notice of Disapproval, if the examiner determines the applicant's skill and abilities to be in serious doubt. 3

In preparation for each practical test, the examiner shall develop a written "plan of action" for each practical test. The "plan of action" is a tool, for the sole use of the examiner, to be used in evaluating the applicant. The plan of action need not be grammatically correct or in any formal format. The plan of action must contain all of the required AREAS OF OPERATION and TASKs and any optional TASKs selected by the examiner. 3

In the previous paragraph, I'm not sure what the FAA means by any optional tasks selected by the examiner. All tasks are required in the PTS and I have not read in any document that gives the examiner freedom to add tasks as they feel necessary.

Maybe the FAA was addressing optional elements. For example the task emergency procedures the examiner selects the emergency procedures he thinks will best meet objective of the task. There are options on what the examiner selects for the procedure but in the end, all elements must be completed (if apply to the aircraft and pilot) to meet the objective and therefore the task is complete.

The "plan of action" shall incorporate one or more scenarios that will be used during the practical test. The examiner should try to include as many of the TASKs into the scenario portion of the test as possible, but maintain the flexibility to change due to unexpected situations as they arise and still result in an efficient and valid test. **Any TASK selected for evaluation during a practical test shall be evaluated in its entirety.** 3

"Any task selected for evaluation during the practical test shall be evaluated in its entirety" can be viewed differently by different examiners. This statement was also bolded in the PTS to add emphasis. As the applicant you need to be prepared to complete every task in its entirety to a conclusion and demonstrate knowledge and proficiency in all of the objectives that apply to you in your aircraft.

Let's look at the task performance and limitations as an example. During the oral exam the examiner is required to complete this task in its entirety, which means the pilot should be prepared with the knowledge and skill required to complete each element. This might be a little bit of a gray area, but if an examiner selects only half of the elements to evaluate a pilot on, did the examiner complete the task in its entirety?

Note: Any equipment inoperative in accordance with a minimum equipment list (MEL) shall be placarded in accordance with the approved MEL procedures and **explained by the applicant** to the examiner describing the procedures accomplished, the resulting operational restrictions, and the documentation for the item(s). 3

Minimum Equipment List

Notice the ATP PTS indicates above that any inoperative equipment will be explained by the applicant. Are you prepared?

The FARs require that all equipment installed on an aircraft in compliance with the airworthiness standards and operating rules be operative. All the aircraft's instruments and equipment, regardless of whether they were essential or not to the flight operation conducted, have to be operative. This is where FAR part 91.213 and a MEL are important because they allow the aircraft be operated with instruments and equipment inoperative.

The best situation is to use an aircraft on the practical test that does not have any inoperative instruments or equipment. This may not always be possible and/or during the practical test a piece of equipment may become inoperative. A pilot must know how to handle the situation using FAR 91.213 or the MEL. If a piece of equipment on the aircraft becomes inoperative during the practical test, and the pilot does not know exactly how to handle this, that pilot will receive a notice of disapproval.

Minimum Equipment List/ Configuration Deviation List

If the aircraft has an approved Minimum Equipment List (MEL), the MEL should be used to determine if a flight may be initiated with inoperative aircraft equipment without the issuance of a special flight permit. The Airplane Flight Manual (AFM) may also include a Configuration Deviation List (CDL) prepared by the manufacturer. If the aircraft does not have an approved MEL, and the aircraft has inoperative equipment or instruments, then the pilot must refer to 14 CFR part 91, section 91.213, to determine if a special flight permit is needed to operate the aircraft.

If the pilot operates the aircraft under FAR part 91 and has an approved MEL, then the applicant should be familiar with how to use the MEL. If the day of the practical test there is any inoperative equipment in the aircraft, the pilot will need to apply the MEL or 91.213.

During the equipment examination under AREA 1 of the PTS it indicates "exhibits satisfactory knowledge of the contents of the Minimum Equipment List (MEL) and/or configuration deviation list (CDL), if appropriate." Notice it does say if appropriate, so if the aircraft does not have an approved MEL or a CDL, I would say the examiner may not ask the pilot questions about this and the pilot should be familiar with 91.213 and how to apply it.

Think about it, if the aircraft does not have a MEL, how can an examiner justify asking a question about another aircraft MEL or ask a pilot how to apply a MEL when the aircraft used does not have one.

Even though everything on the aircraft may be operating, the examiner can give a scenario of what if a piece of equipment was inoperative.

Note: Task Equipment Examination has an objective: "To determine that the applicant" and objective 2 states "exhibits satisfactory knowledge of the contents of the Minimum Equipment List (MEL) and/or configuration deviation list (CDL), if appropriate." Be prepared, to meet this task objective the pilot must exhibit satisfactory knowledge of the MEL or CDL if appropriate.

FAR 91.213 require turbine aircraft to have a MEL and many pilots take ATP practical tests in simulators that are turbine aircraft.

Special Emphasis Areas

After you read the Special Emphasis section of the ATP PTS I think you will agree the examiner must cover the special emphasis areas. This section states the following: "Although these areas may not be specifically addressed under each Task, they are essential to flight safety and will be critically evaluated during the practical test." To be prepared, a pilot should make sure they understand all of the special emphasis areas.

When I read the special emphasis area I read it as the examiner will critically evaluate these areas during the practical test. If the examiner includes all of the PTS special emphasis items, it is a full test and adding more will be difficult. An examiner can't go wrong by including all of the special emphasis items. That way there are no questions about if the examiner did their job.

The examiner may have some freedom to select other areas he feels are critical to flight safety. Based on the explanation of the resource list in the PTS, to be fair to the pilot, the answers to the examiner's choices must be available in the selected resources list in the PTS.

For an example, the special emphasis area of runway incursion avoidance and good cockpit discipline during taxi operations. The examiner can't expect the applicant to do something that he thinks is important to meet the special emphasis area that he cannot reference in any of the references listed in the PTS. For example maybe he learned a good technique for taxi procedures out of a magazine article, but that technique is not in the references of the PTS. He can not expect the pilot to have knowledge of that technique.

Under the task taxiing are the following references:

References:

- Part 61- 61.157 areas of operation

- POH/AFM

- AC 91-73 - Part 91 And Part 135 Single Pilot Procedures During Taxi Operations (24 pages)

- AC 120-57 - Surface Movement Guidance And Control System (62 pages)

- AC 120-74 - Parts 91, 121, 125, And 135 Flightcrew Procedures During Taxi Operations (43 pages)

What do you think would happen if a pilot began taxiing and did not have the airport diagram out and available? Should the examiner fail the pilot? Can the examiner fail the pilot? The ATP PTS under the task taxiing does not indicate the pilot is required to have the airport diagram out and available. The objective of the task taxiing is "to determine that the applicant" and the first objective is "exhibits adequate knowledge of safe taxi procedures (as appropriate to the airplane including push-back or powerback, as may be applicable)."

Now take a look under the reference 91-73A. Located in this document the FAA states "prior to taxiing, a copy of the airport diagram should be available for use by the pilot."

There is a chance that the examiner might fail a pilot who does not have a copy the airport diagram out and available during taxi. The fact that safe taxi operations is a special emphasis area and is also a task indicates the FAA considers it important. The examiner may think that having a copy of the airport diagram available is extremely important but he could fail the pilot because the examiner can reference in one of the references located in the PTS under that task, that the pilot should have an airport diagram available during taxi.

Also in 91-73A: While there may be many views regarding the use of "Airport Diagrams" during taxi operations, the FAA believes that a pilot following the aircraft's progress on the airport diagram to be sure that the instructions received from ATC are being followed is one of the key procedures in reducing runway incursions. This procedure is of particular importance at a time when it is easy to allow oneself to be distracted by outside events.

Finally, from a safety argument, the use of airport diagrams during taxi operations makes perfect sense and should be standard operating procedure for all pilots.

Examiners must place special emphasis upon areas of aircraft operations considered critical to flight safety. Among these are:

1. positive aircraft control;

2. procedures for positive exchange of flight controls;

3. stall/spin awareness;

4. special use airspace and other airspace areas;

5. collision avoidance procedures;

6. wake turbulence and low level wind shear avoidance procedures;

7. runway incursion avoidance and good cockpit discipline during taxi operations; hot spots, and NOTAMs

8. land and hold short operations (LAHSO);

9. controlled flight into terrain (CFIT);

10. aeronautical decision making (ADM)/risk management; and

11. crew resource management/single-pilot resource management (CRM/SRM) to include automation management;

12. recognition of wing contamination to icing;

13. adverse effects of wing contamination in icing conditions during takeoff, cruise, and landing phases of flight;

14. icing procedures of information published by the manufacturer, within the AFM, that is specific to the type of aircraft;

15. traffic awareness, "See and Avoid" concept.

Although these areas may not be specifically addressed under each TASK, they are essential to flight safety and **will be critically evaluated during the practical test.** In all instances, the applicant's actions must relate to the complete situation.

Prior to the test, the examiner must explain, and the applicant must understand, the examiner's role regarding air traffic control (ATC), crew resource management (CRM), and the duties and responsibilities of the examiner through all phases of the practical test. [3]

Practical Test Prerequisites: Airline Transport Pilot

Refer to the current ATP PTS or the FARs.

Practical Test Prerequisites: Aircraft Type Rating

Refer to the current ATP PTS or the FARs.

Aircraft Type Ratings Limited to "VFR ONLY"

Refer to the current ATP PTS.

Removal of the "Limited to Center Thrust" Limitation

Refer to the current ATP PTS.

Aircraft and Equipment Required for the Practical Test

If the practical test is conducted in an aircraft, the applicant is required by 14 CFR part 61 to provide an appropriate and airworthy aircraft for use during the practical test. Its operating limitations must not prohibit the TASKs required on the practical test. Multiengine certification flight checks require normal engine shutdowns and restarts in the air to include propeller feathering and unfeathering. The AFM must not prohibit these procedures. (Low power settings for cooling periods prior to the actual shutdown are acceptable and encouraged as the AFM states.) The exception is for type ratings when that particular airplane was not certificated with inflight unfeathering capability. For those airplanes ONLY, simulated powerplant failures will suffice.

Flight instruments are those required for controlling the aircraft without outside references. The required radio equipment is that which is necessary for communications with ATC, and for the performance of instrument approach procedures. GPS equipment must be instrument certified and contain the current database.

If the practical test is conducted in an aircraft, the applicant is required to provide an appropriate view limiting device that is acceptable to the examiner. The device must be used during all testing that requires testing "solely by reference to instruments." This device must prevent the applicant from having visual reference outside the aircraft, but not prevent the examiner from having visual reference outside the aircraft. A procedure should be established between the applicant and the examiner as to when and how this device should be donned and removed and this procedure briefed before the flight.

The applicant is expected to demonstrate automation management skills in utilizing the autopilot, avionics and systems displays, and/or flight management system (FMS), as applicable to installed equipment, during the practical test to assist in the management of the aircraft. The examiner is expected to test the applicant's knowledge of the systems that are installed and operative during the oral and flight portions of the practical test. This is specifically to include meanings and limitations of airport, taxiway, and runway signs, lights, and markings." 3

Be Prepared

Pilots with limited or no FMS experience do take their ATP/type practical test in aircraft that have a FMS. Pilots in this situation should work with their instructor to focus on the basics of the FMS. A FMS is not something a pilot can learn overnight. They can be complicated and have many great features, but some training courses only give a pilot enough time to learn the basics. Pilots should make sure to understand what the basics are and at a minimum acquire the basic skills needed to operate the FMS. Examples of this are initializing the FMS, inputting a flight plan, setting the FMS for an instrument approach, performance planning, MFD set up, etc.

There are good books and programs available to provide an introduction to FMS operations. A pilot may want to consider this if the training course for the practical test/type is condensed.

How Much Knowledge of the FMS is Enough?

How deep into the FMS can the examiner go? Based on the PTS description above the examiner is expected to test the applicant's knowledge of the systems that are installed and operative during the oral and flight portions of the practical test.

If the aircraft is equipped with a FMS, the operator's manual is required to be in the aircraft. The POH will indicate the FMS manual is required to be in the aircraft. Under the task Preflight Inspection one of the objectives is the pilot exhibits satisfactory knowledge of the operational status of the airplane by locating and explaining the significance and importance of related documents, such as operating limitations, handbooks, and **manuals**. Basically the examiner can ask any question they want from the manual because it is required to be available in the aircraft. Most examiners will ask basic FMS questions, but if a pilot does not know the answer, he should reference the manual. The pilot needs to demonstrate a safe basic understanding of how to operate the FMS.

Here's an example of an aircraft with the Collins FMS-3000 Flight Management System. Located in the POH the pilot should find in the limitations section a requirement that states the following guides must be immediately available to the pilot at all times, and in that list the pilot will find the operator's guide for the Collins FMS-3000 Flight Management System.

Now you might be thinking I am telling you to know the whole FMS operators manual. No, because most pilots and examiners don't have the entire FMS manual memorized. Believe it or not most pilots using FMS equipment know only the basics and there is a lot in the manual still to learn. If a pilot does not know the answer to a particular question, look it up. As long as a pilot can demonstrate satisfactory knowledge, that is what is required to pass. Not have the entire manual memorized.

Day to day flying uses very little of what the FMS is capable of doing. That is why I indicated above a pilot should have a strong basic understanding of the normal functions of a FMS. This is why the FMS manual is required to be aboard the aircraft because when the pilot needs to know something they have not used in the FMS, the pilot will need to reference the manual. During a practical test I think this still applies. You have to ask yourself, if I were flying the airplane and I needed to know a particular piece of information about the FMS that I have never needed to know before, for example a particular message on the FMS, I would reference the manual. But if a pilot does not understand what is considered to be normal basic operation of the FMS, then that can raise a red flag during a practical test. Example, intercepting a course inbound to the fix or using the FMS for RNAV departures.

If during a practical test a pilot is asked a question about the FMS that he has no prior experience with or knowledge of, I think an appropriate answer would be to reference the operators manual which is required to be in the aircraft and accessible to the pilots.

FMS installed, you must know how to use it, at least a strong knowledge of the basics.

If the practical test is conducted in the aircraft and the aircraft has an operable and properly installed GPS, the applicant **must** demonstrate GPS approach proficiency. If the applicant has contracted for training in an approved course that includes GPS training, and the airplane/ simulator/FTD has a properly installed and operable GPS, the applicant **must** demonstrate GPS approach proficiency. When a practical test is conducted for a 14 CFR part 121/135 operator, the operator's approved training program is controlling. [3]

Be Prepared

Conducting GPS approaches is often a confusing task for pilots who do not have any experience with GPS approaches. Again ,this is an area I would recommend preparing for ahead of time by reading books or completing a training program. Most ATP/type courses are conducted in a short period of time and for a pilot to digest all the information required of them plus trying to understand GPS approaches can be overwhelming. Prepare ahead of time.

Actual or Simulated IMC

Note: The applicant must perform the tasks, except for water operations, in actual or simulated instrument conditions unless the practical test cannot be accomplished under instrument flight rules because the aircraft's type certificate makes the aircraft incapable of operating under instrument flight rules. [3]

Most of the practical test will be in actual or simulated instrument conditions. Not all tasks indicate this but this is how it is normally conducted.

I know of examiners who give a visual approach in VFR conditions while completing the task landing form a no flap or a nonstandard flap approach. Based on the above guidance in the PTS this task should be completed in actual or simulated instrument conditions.

Only a few tasks indicate the task must be completed in actual or simulated instrument conditions. They are:

- Precision: Must be accomplished in simulated or actual instrument conditions to DA/DH

- Nonprecision: Indicates in simulated or actual weather conditions. Does not indicate to MDA.

- Circle in simulated or actual instrument conditions to MDA.

- Steep turns indicates in simulated or actual weather conditions.

- Stalls indicates in simulated or actual weather conditions.

- STAR indicates in simulated or actual weather conditions.

- Holding indicates in simulated or actual weather conditions.

Use of an FAA-Approved Flight Simulator or Flight Training Device

The AREA OF OPERATION labeled "PREFLIGHT PREPARATION," the TASKs are knowledge only. These TASKs do not require the use of a flight training device (FTD), flight simulator, or an aircraft to accomplish, **but they may be used**.

Each inflight maneuver or procedure must be performed by the applicant in an FTD, flight simulator, or an aircraft. Appendix 1 of this practical test standard should be consulted to identify the maneuvers or procedures that may be accomplished in an FTD or flight simulator. The level of FTD or flight simulator required for each maneuver or procedure is also found in appendix 1.

When accomplished in an aircraft, certain TASK elements may be accomplished through "simulated" actions in the interest of safety and practicality, **but when accomplished in an FTD or flight simulator, these same actions would not be "simulated."** For example, when in an aircraft, a simulated engine fire may be addressed by retarding the throttle to idle, simulating the shutdown of the engine, simulating the discharge of the fire suppression agent, and simulating the disconnection of associated electrics, hydraulics, pneumatics, etc.

However, **when the same emergency condition is addressed in an FTD or a flight simulator, all TASK elements must be accomplished as would be expected under actual circumstances.** Similarly, safety of flight precautions taken in the aircraft for the accomplishment of a specific maneuver or procedure (such as limiting the altitude in an approach to stall, or setting maximum airspeed for a rejected takeoff) need not be taken when an FTD or a flight simulator is used.

It is important to understand that whether accomplished in an FTD, a flight simulator, or the aircraft, **all TASKs and TASK elements for each maneuver or procedure will have the same performance** criteria applied for determination of overall satisfactory performance. 3

Examiner Responsibility

The examiner who conducts the practical test is responsible for determining that the applicant meets the standards outlined in the Objective of each TASK within the AREAS OF OPERATION in the practical test standard. The examiner must meet this responsibility by determining that the applicant's knowledge and skill meet the Objective in all required TASKs. 3

Complete all Objectives

The examiner must meet the objectives of each task. Most of the tasks have an objective "To determine that the applicant." After the objective is a list of elements for that objective. To meet the objective the examiner must determine the applicant has the knowledge or can demonstrate the skills required for each element. The first element for each task is "exhibits knowledge."

As I have indicated in this book, the examiner must complete each task in its entirety and meet the objective of each task. To meet the objective of each task the examiner must complete each element of that objective that applies to the pilot taking the practical test.

All tasks must be completed and any element that applies must be completed to meet the objective of that task. FAR 61.43 states, an applicant is not eligible for a certificate or rating sought until all the areas of operation are passed.

English Language

In accordance with the requirements of 14 CFR 61.153(b) and ICAO English Language proficiency requirements, the examiner must accomplish the entire application process and test in the English language. The English language component of crew coordination and communication skills can never be in doubt for the satisfactory outcome of the test. Normal restatement of questions as would be done for a native English speaking applicant is still permitted and not grounds for disqualification." 3

Equipment and Flight Exam

The equipment examination in Section 1 must be closely coordinated and related to the flight portion of the practical test in Section 2, but must not be given during the flight portion of the practical test. The equipment examination should be administered prior (it may be the same day) to the flight portion of the practical test. The examiner may accept written evidence of the equipment exam if the exam is approved by the Administrator and administered by an individual authorized by the Administrator. The examiner must use whatever means deemed suitable to determine that the applicant's equipment knowledge meets the standard. 3

The above sentence gives the examiner some freedom in how to determine the applicant's equipment knowledge meets the standard. But the standard is the objective of each task and the elements that it contains. The examiner does not have the freedom to add different objectives or elements to any of the tasks.

Knowledge and Skill Portion of Tasks

The Areas of Operation in Section 2 contain Tasks, which include both "knowledge" and "skill" elements. The examiner must ask the applicant to perform the skill elements. Knowledge elements not evident in the demonstrated skills may be tested by questioning, at anytime, during the flight event. This specifically should include meanings and limitations of airport, taxiway, and runway signs, lights, and markings. Questioning inflight should be used judiciously so that safety is not jeopardized. Questions may be deferred until after the flight portion of the test is completed. 3

Questions During the Flight

If during the flight portion the examiner asks a question to check a pilot's knowledge this is appropriate based on the previous paragraph. The examiner needs to be tactful to not make the questions overly burdensome and distract from the pilot operating the aircraft.

Take a look at each task and typically the first element begins with "exhibits knowledge." Usually the rest of the elements are skill related that must be demonstrated. If the demonstration of skills does not

45

adequately demonstrate the pilots knowledge of the task, the examiner should question the pilot to complete the task.

Basically the way I see it, the PTS is indicating if the pilot demonstrates each element correctly there should not be any questioning. If the examiner is in doubt of the pilot's skill on any of the elements, the examiner should ask questions.

I have heard other examiners and even a FAA inspector basically say that oral questioning should not be conducted in the flight portion of the practical test. The above part of the PTS, gives approval for oral questioning if the examiner deems it necessary because skill or knowledge was not demonstrated.

Oral questioning that is related to Section 1 Preflight Preparation of the ATP PTS is not appropriate in Section 2. An example would be a question during the flight that asks the pilot the maximum fuel the aircraft can hold. This is not appropriate for the flight portion if the question is strictly to quiz the pilot.

An example of a valid oral question during the flight might be, "based on the fuel supply how long would you hold before diverting to the alternate?" The task holding requires the pilot to demonstrate knowledge of holding endurance. If this is not being demonstrated by skill, the examiner can ask to verify knowledge.

As a pilot reviews each task the pilot should focus on the element that requires knowledge and then reference the provided references for that task to ensure adequate knowledge.

One systematic approach to ensuring knowledge is adequate for each individual task is to review the references provided for that task. For example, the task instrument takeoff has some fairly large reference documents. Most of these documents are available in PDF format and provide a method for keyword search. Some tasks will take some effort and some will be completed very quickly. If the applicant prepares ahead of time, I think an applicant can easily keyword search all the available documents.

Examiner Assisting

For aircraft requiring only one pilot, the examiner may not assist the applicant in the management of the aircraft, radio communications, tuning and identifying navigational equipment, or using navigation charts. If the examiner, other than an FAA Inspector, is qualified and current in the specific make and model aircraft that is certified for two or more crewmembers, he or she may occupy a duty position.

If the examiner occupies a duty position on an aircraft that requires two or more crewmembers, the examiner must fulfill the duties of that position. Moreover, when occupying a required duty position, the examiner must perform crew resource management (CRM) functions as briefed and requested by the applicant except during the accomplishment of steep turns and approach to stalls. During these two TASKs the applicant must demonstrate their ability to control the aircraft without the intervention from the non flying pilot.3

8900.1 and CRM

The above statement from the ATP PTS about the examiner not providing CRM during steep turns and stalls is not exactly correct. Located in 8900.1 there is plenty of information contradicting this.

8900.1 Volume 5 seems to send a mixed message. This volume indicates it applies to 121/135 operator's and general aviation based on many of the titles. There is some indication in certain sections that some information may apply to only 121/135 operators. I have to ask why would there be two standards when it comes to an ATP practical test.

8900.1 VOL 5, located under a 121/135/91K section is the following. Inspectors and examiners shall brief supporting crewmembers that they are to perform their duties as specified by the operator's aircraft operating manual. Supporting crewmembers must provide normal crew coordination support; however, they shall not be permitted to lead the applicant when the applicant is expected to take the initiative.

In 8900.1 in a section specifically direct toward142 training centers, there is general information on crew concept that should apply to any practical test. In this section the FAA indicated:

- During a steep turn "the PM provides standard company deviation calls throughout the maneuver."

- This section in 8900.1 also indicates the PM can make power adjustments if specifically requested by the PF. The PF can not request the PM to adjust power to maintain a certain airspeed.

During stall recovery I think it is very acceptable CRM to advance the power levers and direct the PM to "set maximum power." [4]

Safety of Flight

SAFETY OF FLIGHT must be the prime consideration at all times. The examiner, applicant, and crew must be constantly alert for other traffic. [3]

Satisfactory Performance

The ability of an applicant to safely perform the required TASKs is based on:

1. Performing the TASKs specified in the AREAS OF OPERATION for the certificate or rating sought within the approved standards;

2. Demonstrating mastery of the aircraft with the successful outcome of each TASK performed never seriously in doubt (14 CFR section 61.43(a)(2));

3. Demonstrating satisfactory proficiency and competency within the approved standards and single-pilot competence if the aircraft is type certificated for single-pilot operations; and

4. Demonstrating sound judgment and single-pilot resource management/crew resource management. [3]

Never Seriously in Doubt

Definition of seriously is: to a serious degree.

Definition of doubt: regard a successful outcome as unlikely.

61.43(a) (2) does not say "performed never seriously in doubt." 61.43 indicates the pilot must demonstrate mastery of the aircraft by performing each task successfully and demonstrate proficiency and competency within the approved standards.

Demonstrating Sound Judgment

What is the definition of sound judgment. Webster indicates it is the capacity to assess situations or circumstances shrewdly and to draw sound conclusions.

Determining if a pilot has sound judgment can be evaluated starting with the oral exam depending on how the questions are phrased. Definitely judgment should be evaluated during the flight portion of the practical test. I think challenging the pilot's judgment is not done to the extent it should be during practical tests. Especially in the simulator where there is much more freedom to create challenging situations.

Knowledge

"Knowledge" means the applicant can describe in general or specific terms a response to the examiner's question. "Satisfactory knowledge" means the applicant's answer contains at least 70 percent of the reference answer to the examiner's question ("textbook answer") and if the applicant's actions followed his/her response, the safety of the airplane would never be seriously in doubt. [3]

70%

The PTS references at least 70% of the referenced answer. 8900.2 state that it is not uncommon for only one or two incorrect answers to require the issuance of a notice of disapproval during the oral portion of a practical test. It comes down to the questions missed. If the examiner feels that the questions were of such importance that the pilot would not be safe with this level of knowledge, it probably indicates a deficiency that deserves a failure.

I have heard many pilots and instructors think that an applicant can miss 70% of the questions and still pass the practical test. In looking at the different sources of information which are the PTS, 8900.1, 8900.2, this is not specifically stated anywhere. The applicant can miss one question and fail the practical test if that particular question the examiner feels is of such importance that the pilot not knowing the answer is a safety concern.

Unsatisfactory Performance

The tolerances represent the performance expected in good flying conditions. If, in the judgment of the examiner, the applicant does not meet the standards of performance of any TASK performed, the associated AREA OF OPERATION is failed and therefore, the practical test is failed.

Note: The tolerances stated in this standard are intended to be used as a measurement of the applicant's ability to operate in the instrument environment. They provide guidance for examiners to use in judging the applicant's qualifications. The regulations governing the tolerances for operation under Instrument Flight Rules are established in 14 CFR part 91.

The examiner or applicant may discontinue the test at any time when the failure of an AREA OF OPERATION makes the applicant ineligible for the certificate or rating sought. The test may be continued ONLY with the consent of the applicant. If the test is discontinued, the applicant is entitled credit for only those AREAS OF OPERATION and their associated TASKs satisfactorily performed. However, during the retest, and at the discretion of the examiner, any TASK may be reevaluated, including those previously passed. [3]

Typical areas of unsatisfactory performance and grounds for disqualification are:

1. Any action or lack of action by the applicant that requires corrective intervention by the examiner to maintain safe flight.

2. Failure to use proper and effective visual scanning techniques, when applicable, to clear the area before and while performing maneuvers.

3. Consistently exceeding tolerances stated in the Objectives.

4. Failure to take prompt corrective action when tolerances are exceeded. [3]

Clear the Area

If a pilot is taking a practical test in a simulator, the conditions will be IMC and I really don't see the point of clearing the area if the examiner cleared the pilot for the maneuver. If a pilot wants to cover their bases and make sure there is no question, he should ask the examiner if the area is clear or ask the examiner during the brief if it is necessary to clear the area.

Exceeding the Tolerances

The bottom line is that if a pilot exceeds the tolerances stated in the objective get back to the target as soon as possible. Momentary deviations happen and as long as the pilot makes the effort to get back to the target, typically nothing is said. I do have to remind pilots during training, if off the target get back, don't stay off target. Sometimes pilots will hover around the deviation point and for some reason they're not getting back to the target. An example would be if the pilot is 100 feet off altitude on a steep turn. I have seen pilots stay close to that point for some reason and not make an immediate correction back to the assigned altitude.

Never give up! If a pilot feels like they exceeded the tolerances of the maneuver, or did something that's going to cause a failure of the practical test, don't give up and don't say anything. Keep flying the aircraft until the examiner informs you that the task is failed. I've seen too many people verbalize their disappointment in their performance which is only going to draw attention to the deviation. Don't say anything and keep flying. Pilots are very critical of their performance. I've seen pilots complain of their performance when the performance was actually fairly good. Keep flying, don't verbalize or draw any attention to the deviation.

When a Notice of Disapproval is issued, the examiner shall record the applicant's unsatisfactory performance in terms of the AREA OF OPERATION and specific TASK(s) not meeting the standard appropriate to the practical test conducted. The AREA(s) OF OPERATION/

TASK(s) not tested and the number of practical test failures shall also be recorded. If the applicant fails the practical test because of a special emphasis area, the Notice of Disapproval shall indicate the associated TASK. For example, AREA OF OPERATION VI, TASK D, Landing From a Circling Approach, failure to avoid runway incursion. 3

Letter of Discontinuance

When a practical test is discontinued for reasons other than unsatisfactory performance (i.e., equipment failure, weather, illness), The FAA Form 8710-1, Airman Certificate and/or Rating Application, and, if applicable, the Airman Knowledge Test Report, is returned to the applicant. The examiner then must prepare, sign, and issue a Letter of Discontinuance to the applicant. The Letter of Discontinuance must identify the AREAS OF OPERATION and their associated TASKs of the practical test that were successfully completed. The applicant must be advised that the Letter of Discontinuance must be presented to the examiner, to receive credit for the items successfully completed, when the practical test is resumed, and made part of the certification file. 3

Aeronautical Decision Making (ADM) and Risk Management

The examiner must evaluate the applicant's ability throughout the practical test to use good aeronautical decision making procedures in order to evaluate risks. **The examiner must accomplish this requirement by developing scenarios that incorporate as many TASKs as possible to evaluate the applicant's risk management in making safe aeronautical decisions.** For example, the examiner may develop a scenario that incorporates weather decisions and performance planning. Information may be found in AC 60-22, Aeronautical Decision Making, and many other resources as well. 3

Crew Resource Management (CRM and Single Pilot Resource Management (SRM))

CRM/SRM "...refers to the effective use of all available resources: human resources, hardware, and information. Other groups routinely working with the cockpit crew (or single pilot) who are involved in decisions required to operate a flight safely are also essential participants in an effective CRM process. These groups include, but are not limited to: dispatchers, flight attendants, maintenance personnel, flight operations managers, management, pilot examiners, check airmen, flight standards officers, and air traffic controllers." CRM/SRM is not a single TASK. CRM/SRM is a set of competencies, which must be evident in all TASKs in this practical test standard, as applied to the single-pilot or the multicrew operation. CRM focuses on situational awareness, communication skills, teamwork, task allocation, and decision making within a comprehensive framework of standard operating procedures (SOP). SRM is the management of all resources onboard the aircraft and available from outside resources to the single pilot.

CRM/SRM deficiencies almost always contribute to the unsatisfactory performance of a TASK. 3

Poor CRM = Failure

Poor CRM/SRM does contribute to unsatisfactory performance. A pilot needs to make sure while preparing for a practical test that the instructor is critiquing the pilots CRM/SRM skills. If the instructor is not, the pilot needs to ask the instructor to do so. If the instructor is unable to make recommendations or does not seem to have much knowledge about CRM/SRM, the pilot may need to do some research and/or get help from another instructor. This is a very important area and a pilots performance will improve as their CRM/SRM skills are developed.

Scenario Based

Scenario-Based Training and Evaluation. Most accidents are caused by a chain of errors that build up over the course of a flight and which, if undetected or unresolved, result in a final, fatal error. Traditional training programs, with their maneuver-based training and evaluation, artificially segment simulation events in such a way as to prevent the realistic buildup of the error chain. Pilots should ensure the instructor is using scenario-based training during preparation for a practical test.

Most accidents are caused by errors of judgment, communication, and crew coordination. Traditional training programs focus primarily on flying skills and systems knowledge. Expect the examiner to have scenarios to use during the practical test to evaluate a pilots CRM/SRM. A pilot should be prepared to handle the scenarios as PIC. Pilots should not feel they can turn to the examiner at any point during the practical test and ask his opinion. The exception may be if the examiner has previously agreed to act as part of the crew in an aircraft requiring two pilots. Even then the examiner may play dumb to evaluate the pilot. 3

Standard Operating Procedures

A pilot should have their own standard operating procedures. If a pilot is taking an ATP/type practical test in a 121/135/91K environment the operator already has standard operating procedures that the pilot must operate under. Many pilots taking their practical test are operating in the general aviation environment where they are not required to have standard operating procedures.

A pilot should develop some of their own standard operating procedures and sometimes these are also called personal minimums. For example a stabilized approach is often part of standard operating procedures. The FAA has made it very clear how it views what a stabilized approach is and there is a very accepted industry standard for this.

If a pilot is experienced they can look back over the years and determine what they think are important standard operating procedures and develop their own list.

Crew Monitoring and Cross-Checking AC120-51e

Several studies of crew performance, incidents, and accidents have identified inadequate flightcrew monitoring and cross-checking as a problem for aviation safety. Therefore, to ensure the highest levels of safety, each flight crewmember must carefully monitor the aircraft's flight path and systems and actively cross-check the actions of other crewmembers. Effective monitoring and cross-checking can be the last line of defense that prevents an accident because detecting an error or unsafe situation may break the chain of events leading to an accident. This monitoring function is always essential, and particularly so during approach and landing when controlled flight into terrain (CFIT) accidents are most common.

During training make a note of any mistake and ask why did that happen? Let me give you an example I see in the simulator sometimes. The pilots receive a clearance to proceed direct to a fix and the PM enters that into the FMS. The PF does not select NAV mode which will enable the automation to proceed direct to the fix but instead remains in heading mode. The PM does not cross check and verify the PF completed the tasks required to comply with a clearance. The crew should analyze this particular mistake. The obvious answer is that better crosschecking and crew monitoring is required. The PF could request the PM to verify the correct flight control panel (FCP) selection occurs during any clearance that acquires a new FCP selection.

Another example is during non-precision approaches where the aircraft is to descend to a minimum descent altitude (MDA). Often when pilots are new to a particular aircraft this required step during a non-precision approach procedure is often missed. The pilots typically figure it out when the aircraft won't leave the selected altitude. Think the aircraft through the air and have this altitude preset before attempting to descend to the MDA. When this happens the pilots should realize again that crosschecking and crew monitoring is not at the level needed and should be improved. One technique might be to instruct the PM that once the inbound course for the approach has been intercepted that the proper MDA be set or next step down altitude is set. Use the trigger point you want. Develop the best crew coordination possible. Mistakes happen for a reason, fix them and develop procedures to minimize the chances of mistakes.

Error Management AC120-51e

It is now understood that pilot errors cannot be entirely eliminated. It is important, therefore, that pilots develop appropriate error management skills and procedures. It is certainly desirable to prevent as many errors as possible, but since they cannot all be prevented, detection and recovery from errors should be addressed in training. Evaluation of pilots should also consider error management (error prevention, detection, and recovery). Evaluation should recognize that since not all errors can be prevented, it is important that errors be managed properly.

If during a practical test a pilot detects an error, the pilot should fix it and keep flying the airplane. Don't get upset and don't draw attention to the error. Obviously if in an airplane the pilot has to fix the problem and keep moving on. I've seen pilots in the simulator almost give up because they were so disappointed in their mistake. If the practical test is being conducted in a simulator, treat the simulator like an airplane and keep flying after an error is detected.

Summary on CRM

What I've seen in the simulator and in the aircraft is that if a pilot really wants to improve their performance, improve CRM/SRM, error management, monitoring skills, communication skills and cross checking skills. The difference between the best performances I see and the worst is not necessarily the pilot's ability to fly the aircraft but it comes down to who has the best CRM/SRM.

For debriefing purposes, an amplified list of CRM competencies, expressed as behavioral markers, may be found in AC 120-51, as amended, Crew Resource Management Training. These markers consider the use of various levels of automation in flight management systems. 3 AC 120-51e is only 27 pages and would be worth reading prior to your practical test.

CRM/SRM evaluations are still largely subjective. Certain CRM competencies are well-suited to objective evaluation. These are the CRM-related practices set forth in the aircraft manufacturer's or the operator's FAA-approved operating or training manuals as explicit, required procedures. The CRM procedures may be associated with one or more TASKs in these practical test standards. Examples include required briefings, radio calls, and instrument approach callouts. The evaluator simply observes that the individual complies (or fails to comply) with requirements. 3

How the Examiner Evaluates CRM/SRM

Examiners are required to exercise proper CRM/SRM competencies in conducting tests, as well as expecting the same from applicants. Pass/Fail judgments based solely on CRM/SRM issues must be carefully chosen since they may be entirely subjective. Those Pass/Fail judgments, which are not subjective, apply to CRM-related procedures in FAA-approved operations manuals that must be accomplished, such as briefings to other crewmembers. In such cases, the operator (or the aircraft manufacturer) specifies what should be briefed and when the briefings should occur. 3

The above paragraph is mainly referencing approved operations manuals in the FAR 121/135/91K operations. There is a lot more freedom when it comes to CRM/SRM in FAR 91 operations.

Briefings Required by the PTS

The examiner may judge objectively whether the briefings should occur. The examiner may judge objectively whether the briefing requirement was or was not met. In those cases where the operator (or aircraft manufacturer) has not specified a briefing, **the examiner shall require the applicant to brief the appropriate items from the following note**. The examiner may then judge objectively whether the briefing requirement was or was not met.

Note: The majority of aviation accidents and incidents are due to resource management failures by the pilot/crew; fewer are due to technical failures. **Each applicant must give a crew briefing before each takeoff/departure and approach/landing.** If the operator or aircraft manufacturer has not specified a briefing, **the briefing must cover** the appropriate items, such as: departure runway, DP/STAR/IAP, power settings, speeds, abnormal or emergency procedures prior to or after reaching decision speed (i.e., V1 or VMC), emergency return intentions, missed approach procedures, FAF, altitude at FAF, initial rate of descent, DA/DH/MDA, time to missed approach, and what is expected of the other crewmembers during the takeoff/DP and approach/landing. If the first takeoff/departure and approach/landing briefings are satisfactory, the examiner may allow the applicant to brief only the changes, during the remainder of the flight. 3

Briefings

I do get questions about what the briefing should contain and this is often because pilots don't prepare for their practical test and review the PTS. The above section does cover the subject thoroughly and does say the pilot must cover the appropriate items and then a list is provided. If a pilot is a part 91 operator I would say develop a briefing with the above items as a minimum and practice it. If a pilot is flying for a part 121 or 135 operator the operations manual should specify what is required for certain briefings.

An effective briefing is interesting and thorough. It addresses coordination, planning, and problems. Although briefings are primarily a captain's responsibility, other crewmembers may add significantly to planning and should be encouraged to do so.

Behavioral Markers for Briefings

- The captain's briefing establishes an environment for open/interactive communications (e.g., the captain calls for questions or comments, answers questions directly, listens with patience, does not interrupt or "talk over," does not rush through the briefing, and makes eye contact as appropriate).

- The briefing is interactive and emphasizes the importance of questions, critique, and the offering of information.

- The briefing establishes a "team concept" (e.g., the captain uses "we" language, encourages all to participate and to help with the flight).

- The captain's briefing covers pertinent safety and security issues.

- The briefing identifies potential problems such as weather, delays, and abnormal system operations.

- The briefing provides guidelines for crew actions centered on standard operating procedures (SOP); division of labor and crew workload is addressed.

- The briefing includes the cabin crew as part of the team.

- The briefing sets expectations for handling deviations from SOPs.

- The briefing establishes guidelines for the operation of automated systems (e.g., when systems will be disabled; which programming actions must be verbalized and acknowledged).

- The briefing specifies duties and responsibilities with regard to automated systems, for the pilot flying (PF) and the pilot monitoring (PM).

The above information is from AC120-51e Crew Resource Management Training and provides some insight into what is included in an effective briefing. Don't take this lightly; examiners are looking for this to be completed correctly. If a pilot is taking a practical test as a single pilot, the pilot can say aloud the briefings to meet the PTS. The pilot can maybe say the briefing silent and announce that the briefing is complete but the examiner may ask the pilot to say the briefing aloud to meet the PTS.

Standard Calls

Situation: A FAR part 61 pilot has an opportunity to participate in training at a 142 training center where the pilot will complete an initial course for an aircraft requiring a type rating. During this same event the pilot will be attempting their ATP practical test. The usual situation is that this pilot will be paired up with another pilot who is completing the same course and these pilots have never flown together.

The 142 training center is required to have in their training materials CRM techniques, profiles, etc. The problem is some instructors will emphasize this and some will not. The pilot will more than likely have to take control the situation to ensure that good CRM will be used between the two pilots.

Standard phraseology is one aspect of good CRM. Using standard phrases is essential to effective crew communication. It allows the pilots to be able to predict what will be verbalized, and when it is not, it can alert the pilot to a possible problem.

Pilots who use standard calls and phraseology have a better situational awareness, more efficient crew coordination, and much less confusion. Standard calls and phraseology can help the pilots make less decision-making errors. As a pilot's workload increases or the severity of the situation increases, standard calls become very important.

Standard calls should consist of the minimum number of words required to communicate the information. Standard calls should be concise, practical, and makes sense. The absence of a standard call can save your practical test by alerting the pilot of a mistake. This could be the indication of a loss of situational awareness, possible system malfunction, or the other crew member is incapacitated. It is not uncommon during training and maybe a practical test for the examiner or instructor to have one crewmember play incapacitated.

The following is a list of events that a pilot should prepare standard callouts for prior to the practical test:

- Engine starting.
- Setting of engine power or thrust setting.
- Takeoff phase.
- Specific callouts for landing gear and slats/flaps operation.
- Checklist usage, initiation, interruptions, completion and resuming a checklist.
- Flight director and autopilot engagement and disengagement. With this also comes standard calls for flight mode annunciation.
- Automation mode engagement. Standard calls for flight mode annunciation acknowledgment.
- When the automation captures a specific phase, for example a localizer, glideslope, etc.
- Altimeter settings.
- Altitude selector callouts.
- Capturing selected altitudes.
- Ground proximity warning and TCAS responses.
- Transfer of the controls.

- Callouts for specific targets on an instrument approach procedure.

- Excessive deviations from a normal flight profile.

- Unstabilized approach.

- Approaching and reaching minimums on an instrument approach procedure.

- Standard callouts for approach lighting and the runway environment insight.

- Loss of visual reference during an approach procedure.

- Go around standard calls.

- Landing roll callouts.

For those pilots who may not have standard calls already in place the above list is a good starting point. Work with the other pilot and develop standard callouts. If taking a practical test as a single pilot, there will be callouts that can be verbalized and if not verbalized the pilot will want to be mentally thinking of them.

Applicant's Use of Checklists

Throughout the practical test, the applicant is evaluated on the use of an appropriate checklist. In crew served airplanes, the applicant as PIC (acting) should coordinate all checklists with the crew to ensure all items are accomplished in a timely manner. The applicant as acting PIC should manage the flight to include crew checklist performance, requiring standard callouts, announcing intentions, and initiating checklist procedures. If the airplane is a single-pilot airplane, the applicant should demonstrate CRM principles described as single pilot resource management (SRM). Proper use is dependent on the specific TASK being evaluated. The situation may be such that the use of the checklist, while accomplishing elements of an Objective, would be either unsafe or impractical, especially in a single-pilot operation. In this case, a review of the checklist after the elements have been accomplished would be appropriate. Use of a checklist should also consider visual scanning and division of attention at all times. 3

A pilot should be deliberate in the use of checklists. Many pilots take practical test in an aircraft that they have minimal experience in. This also means the pilot will have minimal experience using the approved checklist for that aircraft. Pilots should take their time and be deliberate. I've seen many mistakes made by pilots misinterpreting something in a checklist or accidentally omitting an item in the checklists. For example one crew was accomplishing in-flight engine restart, had a checklist interruption and when the pilot returned to the checklist he missed one line, which was opening the fire wall fuel shutoff valve. They couldn't figure out why the engine would not start.

If a pilot is part of a crew, during abnormal checklists it often works fairly well to have the pilot flying take over communications with ATC to minimize the checklist interruptions to the pilot monitoring.

Pilots should take their time and be thorough while completing a checklist. Read the checklist at a normal pace. Why pilots feel the need to hurry up and complete a checklist, I just don't understand, but it does happen. A pilot's job is to complete the checklist, understand the checklist, and be extremely accurate. Pilots are required to complete the checklist in a reasonable amount of time, but typically when pilots do not complete a checklist in a reasonable amount of time it is because they don't understand the checklist.

During training, in preparation for a practical test, anytime a pilot makes a mistake when conducting a checklist, they should ask why did that happen? If the reason is because of trying to complete the checklist too fast, slow down. If the reason is because the pilot doesn't understand the checklist, try to understand all the checklists.

Here's an example of a common error, especially when a pilot is new to a particular aircraft. The pilot fails to call for the appropriate normal checklist, for example the after takeoff checklist. Think about this for a moment from an examiner's viewpoint. According to the PTS, the PIC is to ensure the checklist is called for and completed in a timely manner. One occurrence of this the examiner might be able overlook this if during the remainder of the practical test the pilot consistently calls for the appropriate checklist. But what if there's another occurrence of not calling for and ensuring the checklist is completed. Do you think the examiner should fail the pilot? Most tasks have an element that indicates the PIC should do or ensure the checklist is completed.

Not calling for the checklist actually occurs a reasonable amount during training, especially the pilot that is new to a particular aircraft. I do also see this with pilots that are familiar with a particular aircraft. I think they're two different things going on here. One is that a pilot is not familiar with an aircraft and is task saturated. The other is that the pilot has poor CRM when it comes to ensuring that the checklists are completed.

Like I said, during training I constantly find pilots failing to call for or complete checklists. Don't get sloppy in this area because I think if during the practical test there is a pattern of this, it could jeopardize passing the practical test.

Initiating Normal Checklists

The pilot flying should initiate normal checklists by calling for the appropriate checklist in a crew environment and then read by the pilot monitoring. If any point during the practical test the pilot flying does not initiate a checklist, the pilot monitoring should suggest the initiation of the appropriate checklist.

Low workload phases of flight are the best times to conduct the normal checklists in a timely manner. If a pilot finds themselves trying to conduct a normal checklists in a rushed manner or during a time where interruptions are occurring, this will jeopardize safety and the whole reason for normal checklists.

Workload management is an important factor in effectively initiating and conducting normal checklists.

Conducting Normal Checklists

The typical method for conducting checklist in a crew environment is a challenge and response method. The pilot monitoring who is conducting the normal checklist will challenge the pilot flying for a response. Items of high importance require a response from the pilot flying. Items that are of less importance can also be challenged and responded to by the pilot flying or the pilot monitoring. This is where establishing crew coordination is important and should already be established before the practical test.

If taking a practical test single pilot then it will be a read and do type of checklist.

Here are some tips to enhance checklist CRM:

- The pilot responding to the challenge should only respond after having completed the response to the challenge.

- If completing the response to the challenge is not possible, the pilot responding should state the actual configuration.

- The pilot challenging should wait for a clear and positive response before moving to the next item of the checklist. The pilot challenging should also crosscheck the actions of the responding pilot. I see pilots with all types of experience levels read the challenge and before the pilot responding makes a clear response, the challenging pilot has moved on to the next checklist item. This often leads to mistakes.

- When a checklist is completed, the pilot monitoring who normally is the pilot reading the checklist should state very clearly that the checklist is complete. An example would be "before landing checklist complete." Even as a single pilot it would be advantageous to verbalize this.

Pilot's Handbook of Aeronautical Knowledge and Checklists

The importance of consistent use of the checklist cannot be overstated in pilot training. A major objective in primary flight training is to establish habit patterns that will serve pilots well throughout their entire flying career. Checklists provide a logical and standardized method to operate a particular make and model airplane. Following a checklist reinforces the use of proper procedures throughout all major phases of flight operations.

There are two primary methods of checklist usage, "read and do" and "do and verify."

The read and do method is when the pilot picks up a checklist, refers to an item, and sets the condition. The items for any particular phase of flight would all be accomplished before the checklist is set aside.

Another acceptable method is to set the condition of the items for a particular phase of operation from memory or flow pattern. Then the checklist is picked up and read to verify that the appropriate condition for each item in that phase has been set. It is not wise for a pilot to become so reliant upon a flow pattern that he or she fails to verify with a checklist. Checking important items solely from memory is not an acceptable substitute for checklists.[4]

Preflight

Many pilots are familiar with their aircraft and conduct a preflight by memory. A pilot can do a preflight from memory but at the end, the pilot should verify that each part of the preflight was completed properly with the use of the checklist. For the practical test I would advise conducting the preflight with the checklist in hand.

The PHAK says "the preflight inspection should be performed in accordance with the printed checklist provided by the airplane manufacturer."

Under the task Preflight in the PTS, objective 3 does state that the pilot uses the appropriate checklist. None of the references under the preflight inspection task include specific information about checklist usage but during the practical test a pilot should follow the guidance in the PHAK and any other authoritative document.

If taking a practical test in a simulator, the preflight portion of the practical test will likely be an approved slideshow. From what I have seen many pilots have done this while not using the checklist and doing the preflight from memory. I would say based on the task Preflight Inspection according to objective 3, the pilot should have open and use the appropriate checklist. If the pilot does not use the appropriate checklist during the preflight inspection objective 3 is not completed and therefore the task is not completed in its entirety.

Checklist Interruption

During the practical test there's a very likely chance that a normal or abnormal checklist will be interrupted. When this occurs the pilot flying should state something along the line of "hold or stop checklist at (specific item)."

After the interruption the pilot flying should state "resume or continue checklist at (specific item)."

The pilot conducting the checklist should resume at the last completed item and repeat that item again. This overlap will help prevent an item from being missed. I've seen more than one crew or individual pilot resume a checklist at the incorrect point and miss an item in the checklist.

Example: Recently I was conducting a simulator training event for two FAR part 135 pilots. Between the two pilots they had almost 15,000 hours and 10 type ratings. Both pilots had been performing very well. Both pilots had a good attitude towards safety and took a lot of pride in being professional.

I gave them an electrical bus short that I don't think they had seen before. They were handling the malfunction well and conducted the checklists in a proper manner. They did not reference the POH to determine all of the items that no longer worked due to the short.

One of the items that no longer worked were the flaps. The PM selected approach flaps and said the flaps were selected but did not check the flap indication. He did the same thing for full flaps after the PF called for full flaps. The PF was very busy flying the aircraft because the autopilot was not functioning properly so he did not notice the flap indication. The crew landed with the flaps in the up position.

After landing the PF did admit he was missing targets like airspeed and normal power settings on final but he did not investigate the reason. The PM was disappointed he made this mistake and said he is normally so adamant about selecting a switch or lever and verifying the system worked correctly.

Anytime the sequence of events is not the normal sequence the likelihood of a normal checklist mistake is much higher.

Some Reasons a Checklist Error Can Occur:

- Instructors during training did not emphasize the importance of strict adherence to normal checklists.

- During high workload times or with an abnormal situation the pilot has a reduced attention because their attention is being divided among other events.

- Poor CRM techniques where there is no crosscheck with other crewmembers, lack of coordination, etc.

- Relying too much on memory.

- Checklist content is not the most effective and/or format of the checklist is not effective. The pilot needs good systems understanding to properly complete some checklist.

- Pilot does not manage priorities very well.

- Checklist interruptions.

- Distractions.

- High level of task saturation, task overload.

- Anytime the sequence of events is not the normal sequence the likelihood of a normal checklist mistake is much higher. [1]

Use of Distractions During Practical Tests

Numerous studies indicate that many accidents have occurred when the pilot has been distracted during critical phases of flight. To evaluate the pilot's ability and situational awareness to utilize proper control technique while dividing attention both inside and outside the cockpit, the examiner must cause a realistic distraction during the flight portion of the practical test to evaluate the applicant's ability to divide attention while maintaining safe flight. [3]

Positive Exchange of Flight Controls

During the flight, there must always be a clear understanding between the pilots of who has control of the aircraft. Prior to flight, a briefing should be conducted that includes the procedure for the exchange of flight controls. Some operators have established a two-step procedure for exchange of flight controls. A popular three-step process in the exchange of flight controls between the pilots is explained below. Any safe procedure agreed to by the applicant and the examiner is acceptable. 3

When one pilot wishes to give the other pilot control of the aircraft, he or she will say, "You have the flight controls." The other pilot acknowledges immediately by saying, "I have the flight controls." The first pilot again says, "You have the flight controls." When control is returned to the first pilot, follow the same procedure. A visual check is recommended to verify that the exchange has occurred. There should never be any doubt as to who is flying the aircraft. 3

Try for 100% Aircraft Monitoring

Positive exchange of flight controls reduces the chance of a practical test failure. Example, a pilot is taking their ATP practical test in an aircraft equipped with a FMS. The pilot believes that when they are the pilot flying, FMS inputs should be completed by the pilot flying because that is part of flying the aircraft just like the flight control panel. If the pilot monitoring is getting approach charts ready and the pilot flying looks down at the FMS to make an input, is either pilot flying the aircraft? If at any point both pilots are looking at something other than monitoring the aircraft, no pilot is flying the aircraft.

Is it impossible for a pilot to be monitoring the aircraft almost the entire flight? I believe it is possible with the proper exchange of flight controls. All duties in the cockpit can be completed in a timely manner and almost 100% of the flight or practical test a pilot can be monitoring the aircraft. It comes down to good CRM and a clear understanding of what is expected and duties.

As PIC, make it your goal to achieve 100% aircraft monitoring during the practical test and any flight. If a practical test is single pilot, this is a slightly different situation. As PIC the pilot will attempt to have minimal heads down time. For example, any time the pilot is reading a checklist or programming the FMS, the pilot should frequently look up to monitor the aircraft and look outside if VMC. Any time a pilot's head is down, the pilot is not actively monitoring the aircraft and the greater chance of a mistake. As a single pilot make sure the flight conditions are a low workload phase of flight when other tasks are completed like programming the FMS.

Crew Monitoring and Cross-Checking

Several studies of crew performance, incidents, and accidents have identified inadequate flight crew monitoring and cross-checking as a problem for aviation safety. Therefore, to ensure the highest levels of safety, each flight crewmember must carefully monitor the aircraft's flight path and systems and actively cross-check the actions of other crewmembers. Effective monitoring and cross-checking can be the last line of defense that prevents an accident because detecting an error or unsafe situation may break the chain of events leading to an accident (or failure of a practical test). This monitoring function is always essential, and particularly so during approach and landing when controlled flight into terrain (CFIT) accidents are most common. AC120-51e

SECTION 1
Preflight Preparation

The Oral Exam

Section 1 Preflight Preparation is the oral exam. The equipment examination in Section 1 must be closely coordinated and related to the flight portion of the practical test in Section 2, but must not be given during the flight portion of the practical test. The equipment examination should be administered prior (it may be the same day) to the flight portion of the practical test.

"Satisfactory knowledge" means the applicant's answer contains at least 70 percent of the reference answer to the examiner's question ("textbook answer") and if the applicant's actions followed his/her response, the safety of the airplane would never be seriously in doubt.

It is not uncommon for only one or two incorrect answers to require the issuance of a notice of disapproval during the oral portion of a practical test. For example, an applicant may be asked a scenario type of question to explain his/her actions on a cross-country flight. If the applicant were to state that an ATC clearance is not required for operation in Class B airspace then it may be appropriate for an Examiner to allow the applicant to complete his/her explanation. The examiner should then follow up with another scenario kind of question about operations into Class B airspace to determine whether the applicant's knowledge was satisfactory or unsatisfactory. If after that question the examiner is certain that the applicant's knowledge is unsatisfactory or incomplete, then the practical test would be terminated and a notice of disapproval should be issued. This same example could apply to scenario based questions that produce incorrect responses about visual flight rules (VFR) weather minimums, aircraft limitations, etc. 8900.2

References

Under each task a list of available references are provided. In looking at the references little closer I came up with a few questions.

Can an examiner ask any question they would like from any of the references provided in the task? Located in 8900.2, Chapter 7, Designated Pilot Examiner Program, Section 2, Conduct Practical Test/Certification Functions, it states:

The demonstration of aeronautical knowledge consists of a question and answer exchange between the examiner and the applicant. The knowledge which should be tested is identified in the applicable PTS and part 61. Trick questions should be avoided. The correct answers to all questions must be available in the regulations, AFM, or other references listed in the applicable PTS.

Also in 8900.2 it states "the examiner must conduct the practical test in accordance with the appropriate regulations, PTS, operating limitations of the aircraft, and procedures prescribed in the Aircraft Flight Manual (AFM)."

I would also like to point out objective 2 under the task Equipment Examination. It is as follows:

Exhibits satisfactory knowledge of the contents of the POH or AFM with regard to the systems and components listed in paragraph 1. This makes it clear. If you are asked a question that is not in the POH, it is not a valid question.

This can actually reduce a pilot's work load when preparing for the practical test. There is a lot of information available to pilots and many have more detail on a particular subject. For example a maintenance manual will have system information not available in the POH. If the information is not in the POH it is off limits for oral exam questions. This information can be important and a pilot should make every effort to understand as much about the aircraft as possible. But when it comes to trying to understand what is exactly required of a pilot during a practical test, the information provided in the POH/AFM, regulations and the references listed in the PTS are controlling.

At the beginning of the PTS located in Practical Test Standard Concept, under references it is stated that "Publications other than those listed may be used for references if their content conveys substantially the same meaning as the referenced publications." I interpret this statement indicating that other references can be used and the FAA did not

71

want to limit the pilot's available resources. But in 8900.2 as you read previously it is very clear on where the correct answers to all questions must come from. Supporting those answers from other resources is permissible, but questions cannot be formed from any resource available, especially if the information is not in the approved resources.

Located also in the PTS is the list of references. At the beginning of those references is the following statement: "This practical test standard is based on the following references."

Summary

For each task it is very clear what references apply to that particular task. If during the oral exam a pilot is asked a question that is not available in the resources identified in the PTS for that task, the pilot should point this out to the examiner.

The clearest answer to this question is in 8900.2. For standardization purposes, I think this is a very important question that should have been easily answered in the PTS. In my research of the available FAA documents this has been the pattern where the most logical answer to a practical test question is in one document and not in another document. A pilot conducting an ATP practical test at a 142 training center should expect the same standards as the pilot taking a practical test with a designated pilot examiner.

> "The general who wins the battle makes many calculations in his temple before the battle is fought. The general who loses makes but few calculations beforehand."
>
> **–SUN TZU**

Areas of Operation

I. Preflight Preparation

TASK A: EQUIPMENT EXAMINATION

References:

The references listed in TASK A almost all relate to icing conditions. Notice part 91 is not part of the references.

- AC 20-29 - Use Of Aircraft Fuel Anti-Icing Additives (6 pages)

- AC 20-117 - Hazards Following Ground Deicing And Ground Operations In Conditions Conducive To Aircraft Icing (38 pages)

- AC 91-43 - Unreliable Airspeed Indications (2 pages)

- AC 91-51A - Effect Of Icing On Aircraft Control And Airplane Deice And Anti-Ice Systems (9 pages)

- AC 91-74 Pilot Guide - Flight In Icing Conditions (96 pages)

- AC 120-60 - Ground Deicing and Anti-icing Program (23 pages)

- AC 135-17 - Pilot Guide Small Aircraft Ground Deicing (35 pages)

Objective: To determine that the applicant:

1. Exhibits satisfactory knowledge appropriate to the airplane; its systems and components; its normal, abnormal, and emergency procedures; and uses the correct terminology with regard to the following items -

   a. landing gear - extension/retraction system(s); indicators, float devices, brakes, antiskid, tires, nose-wheel steering, and shock absorbers.

   b. powerplant - controls and indications, induction system, carburetor and fuel injection, turbocharging, cooling, fire detection/protection, mounting points, turbine wheels, compressors, deicing, anti-icing, and other related components.

c. propellers - type, controls, feathering/unfeathering, autofeather, negative torque sensing, synchronizing, and synchrophasing.

d. fuel system - capacity; drains; pumps; controls; indicators; crossfeeding; transferring; jettison; fuel grade, color and additives; fueling and defueling procedures; and fuel substitutions, if applicable.

e. oil system - capacity, grade, quantities, and indicators.

f. hydraulic system - capacity, pumps, pressure, reservoirs, grade, and regulators.

g. electrical system - alternators, generators, battery, circuit breakers and protection devices, controls, indicators, and external and auxiliary power sources and ratings.

h. environmental systems - heating, cooling, ventilation, oxygen and pressurization, controls, indicators, and regulating devices.

i. avionics and communications - autopilot; flight director; Electronic Flight Instrument Systems (EFIS); Flight Management System(s) (FMS); Doppler Radar; Inertial Navigation Systems (INS); Global Positioning System/ Wide Area Augmentation System/Local Area Augmentation System (GPS/WAAS/LAAS); VOR, NDB, ILS, GLS, RNAV systems and components; traffic (MLS deleted) awareness/warning/avoidance systems, terrain awareness/warning/alert systems; other avionics or communications equipment, as appropriate; indicating devices; transponder; and emergency locator transmitter.

j. ice protection - anti-ice, deice, pitot-static system protection, propeller, windshield, wing and tail surfaces.

k. crewmember and passenger equipment—oxygen system, survival gear, emergency exits, evacuation procedures and crew duties, and quick donning oxygen mask for crewmembers and passengers.

l. flight controls - ailerons, elevator(s), rudder(s), control tabs, balance tabs, stabilizer, flaps, spoilers, leading edge flaps/slats and trim systems.

m. pitot-static system with associated instruments and the power source for the flight instruments.

2. Exhibits satisfactory knowledge of the contents of the POH or AFM with regard to the systems and components listed in paragraph 1 (above); the Minimum Equipment List (MEL) and/or configuration deviation list (CDL), if appropriate; and the operations specifications, if applicable.

Explained

Let's simplify the equipment examination and what is expected the pilot taking the ATP/type practical test.

The references identified in the task - equipment examination total 209 pages. If a pilot is taking their practical test in a BE-55 Baron, there are obviously some references above that do not apply to the aircraft. Fuel anti-icing additives and information about a ground deicing and anti-icing program probably don't apply and should not be asked. But, questions about how to handle frost on the aircraft and how ice accumulation affects aircraft performance are very likely. Reading through the references, focus on the information that applies to the aircraft being used and type of operation(135 or 91).

If a pilot is a part 91 operator, information directed towards 121 and 135 operators may not provide useful information. Just use common sense when studying the references and focus on information that applies to your specific type of operation. If taking a practical test in an airline environment, most of these of references are fair game. Worst case, a pilot has 209 pages to read.

Part 61 is identified in the references because 61.157 list the areas of operation which are what the PTS is based on. So basically, no study time is necessary for this section. This also applies to part 61 references throughout the remaining tasks of the PTS.

In the POH/AFM for the aircraft will be system descriptions. The system descriptions in the POH/AFM is the basic of what a pilot needs to know to operate the aircraft. Maintenance manuals and pilot training manuals provided by other sources can provide more detailed information. The detailed system information to a certain point can make you a better pilot of a specific aircraft. Knowing pressures and insignificant numbers for example maybe a waste of your time.

Let me give you an example using the King Air 350. In the King Air 350 POH under the systems description for the engine there is no mention of an engine bleed valve or a jet flap. These two mechanical parts of the engine serve a purpose of relieving excess compressed air in the lower rpm range. These systems are completely automatic, there is no check-list related to these systems in the POH, and there is no switch in the cockpit that controls them. Information about these two parts of the engine are contained in the maintenance manual and in pilot training manuals provided by other resources.

Should the examiner ask anything about the engine bleed valve or the jet flap? No the examiner should not. These systems are not part of any information in the resources provided under the equipment examination task. It is nice for a pilot to have an understanding of these engine systems and how they operate. Can understanding these two parts of the engine help a person be a better pilot and make a better decision during an engine malfunction, maybe but unlikely.

Notice objective 2 above does indicate knowledge from operations specifications. This is mainly a knowledge area for 121/135 operators. Since this objective is under the task equipment examination, I would say questions from the operations specifications needs to be related to the objectives under this task. Example, a procedure in your operations specification that indicates the pilots will verify N1 fan rotation during icing conditions prior to starting the engine. This may not be in the POH/AFM.

Time Saver!

Note the following statement under the task Equipment Examination:

Objective 2: "Exhibits satisfactory knowledge of the contents of the POH or AFM with regard to the systems and components listed in paragraph 1." This objective makes it very clear that the equipment examination should only include oral questions form the POH/AFM.

POH: It is a good idea to allow enough time prior to your practical test to thoroughly go through the POH associated with the aircraft from front to back.

"The will to win is important, but
the will to prepare is vital."

–JOE PATERNO

TASK B: PERFORMANCE AND LIMITATIONS

References:

- Part 1 - Definitions

- Part 61- 61.157 areas of operation

- Part 91

- AFD - Airport Facility Directory

- AC20-117 - Hazards Following Ground Deicing And Ground Operations In Conditions Conducive To Aircraft Icing (38 pages)

- AC 91-51A - Effect Of Icing On Aircraft Control And Airplane Deice And Anti-Ice Systems (9 pages)

- AC 91-74 Pilot Guide - Flight In Icing Conditions (96 pages)

- AC 91-79 - Runway Overrun Prevention (39 pages)

- AC 120-27 - Aircraft Weight And Balance Control (71 pages)

- AC 120-60 - Ground Deicing and Anti-icing Program (23 pages)

- AC 135-17 - Pilot Guide Small Aircraft Ground Deicing (35 pages)

- FAA-H-8083-1 - Aircraft Weight and Balance Handbook

- FAA-H-8083-3 - Airplane Flying Handbook

- FAA-H-8083-23 - Seaplane, Skiplane, and Float/Ski Equipped Helicopter Operations Book

- FAA-H-8083-25 - Pilot's Handbook of Aeronautical Knowledge

Objective: To determine that the applicant:

1. Exhibits satisfactory knowledge of performance and limitations, including a thorough knowledge of the adverse effects of exceeding any limitation.

2. Demonstrates proficient use of (as appropriate to the airplane) performance charts, tables, graphs, or other data relating to items, such as –

    a. departure airport, taxiway, and runway NOTAMs, runway usable lengths, HOT Spots, taxi restrictions, specific taxi procedures, as applicable, and signage/markings

    b. accelerate-stop distance.

    c. accelerate-go distance.

    d. takeoff performance - all engines and with engine(s) inoperative.

    e. climb performance including segmented climb performance with all engines operating - with one or more engine(s) inoperative, and with other engine malfunctions as may be appropriate.

f. service ceiling - all engines, with engines(s) inoperative, including drift down, if appropriate.

g. cruise performance.

h. fuel consumption, range, and endurance.

i. descent performance.

j. arrival airport, taxiway, and runway NOTAMs, runway usable lengths, HOT Spots, tax restrictions, specific tax procedures as applicable, and signage/markings.

k. landing distance.

l. land and hold short operations (LAHSO).

m. go-around from rejected landings (landing climb).

n. other performance data (appropriate to the airplane).

3. Describes (as appropriate to the airplane) the airspeeds used during specific phases of flight.

4. Describes the effects of meteorological conditions upon performance characteristics and correctly applies these factors to a specific chart, table, graph, or other performance data.

5. Computes the center-of-gravity location for a specific load condition (as specified by the examiner), including adding, removing, or shifting weight.

6. Determines if the computed center-of-gravity is within the forward and aft center-of-gravity limits, and that lateral fuel balance is within limits for takeoff and landing.

7. Demonstrates adequate knowledge of the adverse effects of airframe icing during pre-takeoff, takeoff, cruise and landing phases of flight and corrective actions.

8. Demonstrates adequate knowledge of procedures for wing contamination recognition and adverse effects of airframe icing during pre-takeoff, takeoff, cruise, and landing phases of

flight. (Pilots applying for an aircraft type rating should have adequate knowledge of icing procedures and/or available information published by the manufacturer that is specific to that type of aircraft.)

9. Demonstrates good planning and knowledge of procedures in applying operational factors affecting airplane performance.

10. Demonstrates knowledge of the stabilized approach procedures and the decision criteria for go-around or rejected landings.

Explained

One way to approach this section is to go through each reference and focus on any information that is related to aircraft performance. All of these can be found in a PDF format which will enable a pilot to do a keyword search. Focus on performance information that applies to your specific aircraft. For example if a pilot was flying a Beechcraft Baron, performance information related to a turbine powered aircraft would not apply to that pilot's practical test.

Thoroughly go through the performance section of the aircraft POH. Understand all of the performance charts, but especially focus on the performance charts listed in this task.

Take a look at objective 9. This is a fairly broad objective and could probably include many types of questions. Objective 9 and 2(d) could include a question like "if an engine failure occurs on takeoff would we clear all obstacles?" "What about the close in obstacles indicated in the A/FD?" "What would you do if an engine failure occurs during takeoff?" If a pilot has not prepared well for the performance section, these questions can be difficult to answer. Would you fail a pilot if they could not figure if the trees at the end of the runway would be cleared if an engine failure occurred? What if the pilot could not determine single engine missed approach performance? What if the pilot could not determine if the aircraft could comply with the climb gradient on a departure procedure?

There are many possibilities for questions in this section. Prepare ahead of time.

"The best preparation for good work
tomorrow is to do good work today."
-ELBERT HUBBARD

NOTE: Task C and D for AMES/ASES, refer to PTS.

SECTION 2:

Preflight Procedures, Inflight Maneuvers, and Postflight Procedures

Areas of Operation

II. Preflight Procedures

TASK A: PREFLIGHT INSPECTION

NOTE: If a flight engineer (FE) is a required crewmember for a particular type airplane, the actual visual inspection may be waived. The actual visual inspection may be replaced by using an approved pictorial means that realistically portrays the location and detail of inspection items. On airplanes requiring an FE, an applicant must demonstrate satisfactory knowledge of the FE functions for the safe completion of the flight if the FE becomes ill or incapacitated during a flight.

References:

- Part 61- 61.157 areas of operation

- Part 91

- POH/AFM

- AC 20-29 - Use Of Aircraft Fuel Anti-Icing Additives (5 pages)

- AC 20-117 - Hazards Following Ground Deicing And Ground Operations In Conditions Conducive To Aircraft Icing (38 pages)

- AC 61-84 - Role Of Preflight Preparation (8 pages)

- AC 91-43 - Unreliable Airspeed Indications (2 pages)

- AC 91-51A - Effect Of Icing On Aircraft Control And Airplane Deice And Anti-Ice Systems (9 pages)

- AC 91-74 Pilot Guide - Flight In Icing Conditions (96 pages)

- AC 120-27 - Aircraft Weight And Balance Control (71 pages)

- AC 120-60 - Ground Deicing and Anti-icing Program (23 pages)

- AC 135-17 - Pilot Guide Small Aircraft Ground Deicing (35 pages)

Objective: To determine that the applicant:

1. Exhibits satisfactory knowledge of the preflight inspection procedures, while explaining briefly-

    a. the purpose of inspecting the items which must be checked.

    b. how to detect possible defects.

    c. the corrective action to take.

2. Exhibits satisfactory knowledge of the operational status of the airplane by locating and explaining the significance and importance of related documents, such as -

    a. airworthiness and registration certificates.

    b. operating limitations, handbooks, and manuals.

    c. minimum equipment list (MEL), if appropriate.

    d. weight and balance data.

    e. maintenance requirements, tests, and appropriate records applicable to the proposed flight or operation; and maintenance that may be performed by the pilot or other designated crewmember.

3. **Uses the appropriate checklist** or coordinates with crew to ensure completion of checklist items in a timely manner and **as recommended by the manufacturer** or approved method to inspect the airplane externally and internally.

4. Verifies the airplane is safe for flight by emphasizing (as appropriate) the need to look at and explain the purpose of inspecting items, such as -

   a. powerplant, including controls and indicators.

   b. fuel quantity, grade, type, contamination safeguards, and servicing procedures.

   c. oil quantity, grade, and type.

   d. hydraulic fluid quantity, grade, type, and servicing procedures.

   e. oxygen quantity, pressures, servicing procedures, and associated systems and equipment for crew and passengers.

   f. hull, landing gear, float devices, brakes, steering system, winglets, and canards.

   g. tires for condition, inflation, and correct mounting, where applicable.

   h. fire protection/detection systems for proper operation, servicing, pressures, and discharge indications.

   i. pneumatic system pressures and servicing.

   j. ground environmental systems for proper servicing and operation.

   k. auxiliary power unit (APU) for servicing and operation.

   l. flight control systems including trim, spoilers, and leading/ trailing edge.

   m. anti-ice, deice systems, servicing, and operation.

n. installed and auxiliary aircraft security equipment, as appropriate.

5. Coordinates with ground crew and ensures adequate clearance prior to moving any devices, such as door, hatches, and flight control surfaces.

6. Complies with the provisions of the appropriate operations specifications, if applicable, as they pertain to the particular airplane and operation.

7. Demonstrates proper operation of all applicable airplane systems.

8. Notes any discrepancies, determines if the airplane is airworthy and safe for flight, or takes the proper corrective action, and acknowledges limitations imposed by MEL/CDL items.

9. Checks the general area around the airplane for hazards to the safety of the airplane and personnel.

10. Ensures that the airplane and surfaces are free of ice, snow, and has satisfactory knowledge of deicing procedures, if icing conditions were present or ice was found.

Explained

A pilot should review line by line the preflight section of the POH/AFM and understand each line of the preflight and be able to explain it. Understanding each expanded checklist if one is available. Be sure to understand any information in the aircraft system section of the POH if it relates to the preflight.

This is one of the sections that a pilot may be asked an odd question and being able to understand what is expected of you is important. For example, what if the examiner asks what a particular antenna is on the bottom of the aircraft. If it's not identified in the preflight section of the POH and is not identified in the system section of the POH then a pilot really does not need to know what kind of antenna it is. It would be nice to know, but I would have to say it's not really required because the information is not available in the references provided for the task preflight inspection. A pilot can answer the question with, "I will have to ask maintenance or do some further research in the maintenance manuals or even that is not a valid question for the preflight task." Notice the maintenance manual is not part of the references.

What if pilot is asked how many static wicks are on the aircraft? What if that information is not in the preflight section of the POH? What if it is not in the systems section of the POH? It could be in the equipment list of the POH and/or in the MEL. The answer might be, show me a picture or let me look at the aircraft and I will tell you. The pilot could say "I will have to look up that information in the POH because it is not listed in the prefight checklist." Obviously if it is in the preflight checklist that is easy.

This type of question may be one of those gray areas of knowledge. Sure it is probably important to know how many static wicks are located on a particular surface so it would easily be noticed if one is missing. But if that information is not located in the POH or the checklist, how can a pilot be held accountable for that type of information. If the POH indicates to check the static wicks, that is what it means. If the POH indicates 6 static wicks should be on the wing, then that is what it is. There is no requirement to remember how many static wicks are on the aircraft. Go to the appropriate resource and find out how many are required.

If the preflight portion of the practical test will not be conducted with the actual airplane, it will be conducted with an FAA approved pictorial aircraft preflight inspection. According to objective 3 of this task, the pilot should conduct the preflight using the appropriate checklist. The pilot should not have to conduct the preflight strictly by memory.

According to FAA 8900.1, Volume 3, Chapter 54 for 142 Training Centers, the preflight procedures contained in the FAA-approved Aircraft Flight Manual (AFM) or Rotorcraft Flight Manual (RFM) is the standard references for the preflight visual inspection. They are primary for determining essential preflight items and the sequence in which those items should be inspected. 4

Use the appropriate checklist. The answer to any question during this task is there. Some answers could be in the systems section of the POH.

The preflight is not part of the task equipment examination. There should be no questions that resemble the equipment examination.

Example King Air preflight. When the pilot preflights the engine area, the checklist states, collector drain - clear. If the examiner asks, what are you checking here. The answer is that it is clear. During the preflight task the examiner should not ask a question like, what is the purpose of the collector drain? In fact even during the equipment examination this is not a valid question because the collector drain is not mentioned in the systems section of the POH.

Another example that may not be as clear as the collector drain. During the same preflight the pilot will check the engine oil. The preflight checklist states, engine oil – check quantity, cap secure. In this case the pilot should expect the examiner to ask a question to meet objective 1 and 4. The question might be - what is the normal operating range of the oil? This answer can be found in the POH under the General section. He may ask, if you had to add oil what type would you put in? The answer again is in the POH under the General and Handling, Service and Maintenance section but may also require talking with maintenance or getting more information like from a service bulletin. He may ask what is the maximum quantity of the oil system? Again the answer is in the POH. If you have any of these answers memorized, great, but referring to the POH is acceptable and on some subjects shows great decision making. Pilots can't remember everything and referring to proper guidance like the POH should be done more.

The King Air POH under Handling Service and Maintenance with reference to oil it states - before servicing the airplane with engine oil, obtain the latest copy of Pratt and Whitney SB 13001. Only those engine oils listed in P&WC Service Bulletin 13001 are to be used in the PT6A-60A engines. Do not mix different oil brands together.

If the pilot does not have the service bulletin available in the aircraft, nothing should be done until it is obtained or the pilot speaks with maintenance.

Hopefully these couple of examples gives you some idea on what is expected of the pilot. Refer to the POH if you don't know the answer.

> "The meeting of preparation with opportunity
> generates the offspring we call luck."
> **—TONY ROBBINS**

TASK B: POWERPLANT START

References:

- Part 61- 61.157 areas of operation

- POH/AFM

Objective: To determine that the applicant:

1. Exhibits adequate knowledge of the correct powerplant start procedures including the use of an auxiliary power unit (APU) or external power source, starting under various atmospheric conditions, normal and abnormal starting limitations, and the proper action required in the event of a malfunction.

2. Ensures the ground safety procedures are followed during the before-start, start, and after-start phases.

3. Ensures the use of appropriate ground crew personnel during the start procedures.

4. Performs all items of the start procedures by systematically following the approved checklist procedure in a timely manner and as recommended by the manufacturer for the before-start, start, and after-start phases.

5. Demonstrates sound judgment and operating practices in those instances where specific instructions or checklist items are not published.

Explained

Understand thoroughly what is the appropriate action during the engine start procedure and starts with malfunctions. These procedures are often not identified as items the pilot is required to memorize, but a thorough understanding does require the pilot to memorize them.

For example a hot start on a turbine engine requires immediate action by the pilot.

Be careful not to overlook the external power starting procedures and associated limitations.

After any start malfunction in a crewed flight deck call for the appropriate checklist and in a single pilot operation complete the appropriate checklist.

FAR 91.503 for large and turbine powered multiengine aircraft must have a cockpit checklist with certain procedures. These procedures like "before starting engines" shall be used by the flight crew. Notice it is not starting engines and that is not part of the list. If the manufacture has provided a starting engines checklist, use it.

Note that part 91 is not one of the references but is part of the PTS reference list and can be referenced by the examiner.

Note objective 4, it is very clear the pilot should use the checklist for this task.

Take a look at objective 2. There are only two references in this task and the only reference that may contain some information about ground safety procedures is the POH/AFM. In the reference list, there are a few that provide guidance like the FAA handbooks and the AIM.

Based on all of the guidance the examiner can expect a pilot to meet objective 2 by using guidance in any reference in the complete PTS list, not just the task reference list.

"One important key to success is
self-confidence. An important key to
self-confidence is preparation."
–ARTHUR ASHE

TASK C: TAXIING

References:

- Part 61- 61.157 areas of operation

- POH/AFM

- AC 91-73 - Part 91 And Part 135 Single Pilot Procedures During Taxi Operations (24 pages)

- AC 120-57 - Surface Movement Guidance And Control System (62 pages)

- AC 120-74 - Parts 91, 121, 125, And 135 Flight Crew Procedures During Taxi Operations (43 pages)

Objective: To determine that the applicant:

1. Exhibits adequate knowledge of safe taxi procedures (as appropriate to the airplane including push-back or power-back, as may be applicable).

2. Demonstrating and explaining procedures for holding the pilot's workload to a minimum during taxi operations .

3. Exhibiting taxi operation planning procedures, such as recording taxi instructions, reading back taxi clearances, and reviewing taxi routes on the airport diagram.

4. Demonstrating procedures to insure that clearance or instructions that are actually received are adhered to rather than the ones expected to be received.

5. Know, explain and discuss the hazards of low visibility operations.

6. Demonstrates proficiency by maintaining correct and positive airplane control. In airplanes equipped with float devices, this includes water taxiing, sailing, step taxiing, approaching a buoy, and docking.

7. Maintains proper spacing on other aircraft, obstructions, and persons.

8. Accomplishes the applicable checklist items or ensures all required checks as required by the appropriate checklist items are accomplished in a timely manner and as recommended by the manufacturer, and performs recommended procedures.

9. Maintains desired track and speed.

10. Complies with instructions issued by ATC (or the examiner simulating ATC).

11. Observes runway hold lines, localizer and glide slope critical areas, buoys, beacons, and other surface control and lighting.

12. Maintains constant vigilance and airplane control during taxi operation to prevent runway/waterway incursion.

13. Demonstrating and/or explaining procedural differences for night operations.

14. Demonstrating and explaining the use(s) of aircraft exterior lighting and differences for day and night operations.

Explained

If a pilot is taking the practical test as a single pilot, I would recommend and I think best practice is to not do any systems checks while taxiing. Objective 8 requires the pilot to maintain a constant vigilance and airplane control during taxi operation. This is hard to do with your head down at any point.

AC 91.73A states pilots should perform heads down tasks (e.g., programming the FMS, calculating takeoff data) while the aircraft is stopped.

In a simulator if the examiner has not specified where to do run-up procedures, simulate contacting ground control to request taxi to a run-up area. Obvious in the actual aircraft the pilot should be aware what location is best suited for run-up procedures. In a simulator there is a little more freedom, but it shows good decision-making when the pilot requests taxi to a run-up area.

Speed Control

Unless the POH/AFM indicates a taxi speed the above references do not discuss speed management, steering, or maneuvering the aircraft, but do suggest some good practices regarding other cockpit activities during taxi. Proper taxi speed is up for interpretation. As long as a pilot maintains good control of the aircraft, speed is up for interpretation.

A keyword search of taxi speed in the AIM produces no real results.

Night

The PTS now includes objectives under the tasks Taxiing and After Landing Procedures that includes night operations. Be prepared to answer questions on these objectives if the practical test is conducted during the day. In the simulator the examiner can make it night operations to meet these objectives. Notice there is no exception to the objectives, the examiner must cover them.

"Luck is a matter of preparation meeting opportunity."

–LUCIUS ANNAEUS SENECA

TASK F: PRE-TAKEOFF CHECKS

References:

- Part 61- 61.157 areas of operation

- POH/AFM

- AC 91-74 - Pilot Guide Flight In Icing Conditions (96 pages)

- AC 120-60 - Ground Deicing and Anti-icing Program (23 pages)

- AC 20-117 - Hazards Following Ground Deicing And Ground Operations In Conditions Conducive To Aircraft Icing (38 pages)

Objective: To determine that the applicant:

1. Exhibits satisfactory knowledge of the pre-takeoff checks by stating the reason for checking the items outlined on the approved checklist and explaining how to detect possible malfunctions.

2. Divides attention properly inside and outside cockpit.

3. Ensures that all systems are within their normal operating range prior to beginning, during the performance of, and at the completion of those checks required by the approved checklist.

4. Explains, as may be requested by the examiner, any normal or abnormal system-operating characteristic or limitation; and the corrective action for a specific malfunction.

5. Determines if the airplane is safe for the proposed flight or requires maintenance.

6. Determines the airplane's takeoff performance, considering such factors as wind, density altitude, weight, temperature, pressure altitude, and runway/waterway condition and length.

7. Determines airspeeds/V-speeds and properly sets all instrument references, configures flight director and autopilot controls, and navigation and communications equipment to properly fly the aircraft in accordance with the ATC clearance.

8. Reviews procedures for emergency and abnormal situations, which may be encountered during takeoff, and states the corrective action required of the pilot in command and other concerned crewmembers.

9. Obtains and correctly interprets the takeoff and departure clearance as issued by ATC.

Explained

A pilot should understand all of the pre-takeoff checks related to the aircraft. Be able to explain each checklist item in general terms. It is interesting that objective 1 indicates that the pilot is to state the reason for checking the items. Be prepared, your examiner can ask you to do this.

For each system that is being checked, a pilot should understand what are the possible malfunctions with that system. For example, if checking the propeller primary governor system, the pilot should understand how to detect a primary governor failure.

If a pilot is taking a practical test in a simulator, how many malfunctions are appropriate during the pre-takeoff checks? So far I have not found any guidance on this question. Most examiners will give 3 to 5 malfunctions during the pre-takeoff checks. If the goal as stated in the practical test guidance and examiner information is to create scenarios, this many malfunctions destroys the scenario because it is unrealistic. Giving a pilot one malfunction during the preflight checks, leading the pilot to use the MEL or apply 91.213, use good decision-making skills in determining whether the flight can continue or not is maybe a better evaluation. Evaluating whether the pilot catches multiple malfunctions does not necessarily evaluate aeronautical decision-making but it does evaluate system knowledge. System malfunctions can be part of the task Equipment Examination and maybe keep the flight as realistic as possible.

According to objective 4 the examiner can request the pilot to explain any normal or abnormal system-operating characteristic or limitation; and the corrective action for a specific malfunction. In completing this objective multiple malfunctions might be appropriate but again it still may take away from the scenario. Maybe the best scenario is to have one malfunction the pilot deals with and the examiner asks knowledge questions.

Objective 3 requires the pilot to ensure all systems are normal. This objective indicates the pilot is to complete all checks in the approved checklist. If the examiner shortens the checklist at all, the objective is not met.

During the pre-takeoff checks don't forget that every piece of equipment on the aircraft must be operating. If a piece of equipment is not operating, the pilot must apply the MEL if appropriate or apply 91.213 inoperative instruments and equipment.

"Before anything else, preparation
is the key to success."
–ALEXANDER GRAHAM BELL

III. Takeoff and Departure Phase

TASK A: NORMAL AND CROSSWIND TAKEOFF

References

- Part 61- 61.157 areas of operation

- POH/AFM

- FAA-H-8083-3 - Airplane Flying Handbook

- AC 20-117 - Hazards Following Ground Deicing And Ground Operations In Conditions Conducive To Aircraft Icing (38 pages)

- AC 91-54 - Automatic Reporting Systems – Altimeter Setting And Other Operational Data (10 pages)

- AC 91-74 - Pilot Guide – Flight In Icing Conditions (96 pages)

Note: VMC maneuver.

Objective: To determine that the applicant:

1. Exhibits knowledge of normal and crosswind takeoffs and climbs including (as appropriate to the airplane) airspeeds, configurations, and emergency/abnormal procedures.

2. Notes any surface conditions, obstructions, aircraft cleared for LAHSO, or other hazards that might hinder a safe takeoff.

3. Verifies and correctly applies correction for the existing wind component to the takeoff performance.

4. Coordinates with crew (if crew served airplane) to ensure completion or completes required checks prior to starting takeoff to verify the expected powerplant performance. Performs or ensures all required pre-takeoff checks as required by the appropriate checklist items are accomplished in a timely manner and as recommended by the manufacturer.

5. Aligns the airplane on the runway centerline or clear of obstacles and vessels on waterways as appropriate.

6. Applies the controls correctly to maintain longitudinal alignment on the centerline of the runway, if appropriate, prior to initiating and during the takeoff.

7. Adjusts the powerplant controls as recommended by the FAA-approved guidance for the existing conditions.

8. Monitors powerplant controls, settings, and instruments during takeoff to ensure all predetermined parameters are maintained.

9. Adjusts the controls to attain the desired pitch attitude at the predetermined airspeed/V-speed to attain the desired performance for the particular takeoff segment.

10. Performs the required pitch changes and, as appropriate, performs or calls for and verifies the accomplishment of, gear and flap retractions, power adjustments, and other required pilot-related activities at the required airspeed/V-speeds within the tolerances established in the POH or AFM.

11. Uses the applicable noise abatement and wake turbulence avoidance procedures, as required.

12. Accomplishes, or calls for and verifies the accomplishment of, the appropriate checklist items in a timely manner and as recommended by the manufacturer.

13. Maintains the appropriate climb segment airspeed/V-speeds.

14. Maintains the desired heading, ±5°, and the desired airspeed (V-speed), ±5 knots (of the appropriate V-speed range).

Explained

Be sure to apply the correct crosswind flight control input. I do see a lot of pilots forget to do this.

Refer to the POH to determine the recommended method of setting the power and beginning the takeoff roll. Some aircraft require the brakes to be held, takeoff power set and then the brakes released. The POH of some aircraft makes no allowance for a rolling takeoff. If the aircraft POH does not approve a rolling takeoff, you are opening the opportunity for questioning.

Here's how the examiner may view a rolling takeoff in an aircraft where the POH does not give approval or guidance for a rolling takeoff. Does the pilot not understand the performance of the aircraft or is the pilot ignoring it? The performance numbers calculated by the pilot for that particular takeoff are now invalid. The examiner will probably ask questions to determine if the objective of this task is being met.

Example, the Citation 560XL POH approves adding 500 feet to the takeoff field length required if a pilot executes a rolling takeoff. The King Air 350 at the beginning of the performance section for dry runway conditions indicates the pilot shall hold the brakes, set takeoff power and then begin the takeoff roll. Nothing in the King Air POH provides a factor to be applied for a rolling takeoff on a dry runway.

When it comes to setting takeoff power, set what the POH/AFM indicates should be set for those particular conditions. In some aircraft, as the aircraft rolls down the runway the takeoff power that was set prior to brake release will increase slightly. This is factored in the takeoff performance and more than likely should be left alone unless stated differently in your POH/AFM. An example of this is setting takeoff torque in a turbo propeller airplane. Let's say the takeoff torque setting under certain conditions was 95% torque. During the takeoff roll the torque will increase. A technique applied by many pilots is setting about 5% less than what the POH/AFM indicates should be set. If the POH does not indicate this is an approved procedure, don't do it. Should the examiner accept this? It is a procedure that is not supported in the POH/AFM and technically the performance that the pilot determined in the oral exam is invalid.

Another point to make here is that during the certification part of the aircraft under part 23, the increase in torque that occurs is factored into the performance.

Not setting takeoff power as indicated by the POH/AFM will give the examiner grounds for failing the pilot on this task due to not complying with objectives 7 and 8 or force him to apply oral questioning to verify the pilots knowledge and understanding.

The bottom line is study the POH/AFM performance section and understand the airplane and how the manufacture determines the aircraft performance.

Understand what are the appropriate climb airspeeds. A pilot may have a particular climb airspeed they prefer that is different from the profile airspeeds in the POH. I would recommend a pilot at least be able to explain why they prefer a certain climb speed as opposed to the airspeeds designated in the POH/AFM. When I ask pilots what airspeed they are trying to maintain in the climb, I sometimes get a very vague answer that indicates to me that they really don't have a target airspeed or understand the performance section of the POH.

Be sure to call for the appropriate after takeoff checklist or if single pilot execute the checklist at a safe altitude and phase of flight. During single pilot operations don't feel that the checklist has to be completed immediately after takeoff. Climb to a safe altitude.

This task had a note about this being a VMC maneuver. Visual meteorological conditions. All of the takeoffs can not be instrument takeoffs. This task does not indicate it can be combined with the task Instrument Takeoff. It can be combined with the task Powerplant Failure During Takeoff. Very few examiners in the simulator are giving the engine failure during takeoff in VMC conditions, but they can.

"There is no short cut to achievement.
Life requires thorough preparation—
veneer isn't worth anything."
–GEORGE WASHINGTON CARVER

TASK E: INSTRUMENT TAKEOFF

References

- Part 61- 61.157 areas of operation

- POH/AFM

- AIM

- FAA-H-8083-15 - Instrument Flying Handbook

- FAA-H-8261-1 - Instrument Procedures Handbook

- AC 20-117 - Hazards Following Ground Deicing And Ground Operations In Conditions Conducive To Aircraft Icing (38 pages)

- AC 91-74 - Pilot Guide – Flight In Icing Conditions (96 pages)

- AC 135-17 - Pilot Guide Small Aircraft Ground Deicing (35 pages)

Objective: To determine that the applicant:

1. Exhibits knowledge of an instrument takeoff with instrument meteorological conditions (IMC) simulated at or before reaching an altitude of 100 feet AGL. If accomplished in a flight simulator, visibility should be no greater than one quarter (1/4) mile, or as specified by operator specifications, whichever is lower.

2. Takes into account, prior to beginning the takeoff, operational factors which could affect the maneuver, such as Takeoff Warning Inhibit Systems or other airplane characteristics, runway length, surface conditions, wind, wake turbulence, icing conditions, obstructions, and other related factors that could adversely affect safety.

3. Coordinates with crew, if a crew served airplane, or completes the appropriate checklist items in a timely manner and as recommended by the manufacturer in a single pilot airplane, to

ensure that the airplane systems applicable to the instrument takeoff are operating properly.

4. Sets the applicable avionics and flight instruments to the desired setting prior to initiating the takeoff.

5. Applies the controls correctly to maintain longitudinal alignment on the centerline of the runway, if appropriate, prior to initiating and during the takeoff.

6. Transitions smoothly and accurately from visual meteorological conditions (VMC) to actual or simulated instrument meteorological conditions (IMC).

7. Maintains the appropriate climb attitude.

8. Complies with the appropriate airspeeds/V-speeds and climb segment airspeeds.

9. Maintains desired heading within ±5° and desired airspeeds within ±5 knots.

10. Complies with ATC clearances and instructions issued by ATC (or the examiner simulating ATC).

11. Acknowledges and makes appropriate callouts to coordinate with the crew, if in a crew served airplane.

Explained

Operating an aircraft in low visibility conditions is a complicated procedure. A pilot should make sure they understand how to setup all applicable avionics and flight instruments for this type of takeoff.

In the actual aircraft and in conditions not less than instrument conditions, expect the examiner to put on the view limiting device prior to reaching 100 feet AGL.

In the simulator expect the RVR to be set to a low value and the ceiling at 100 feet AGL.

Tip, never launch an IFR flight without obtaining current visibility information immediately prior to departure. Ask ATC(examiner) what the visibility is prior to takeoff.

Tip, aircraft operating under part 91 are not required to comply with established takeoff minimums. Legally, a zero/zero departure may be made, but it is never advisable. Your examiner might ask if you would takeoff with a visibility less than that required. Part 91, you decide what is the best decision.

Notice a few of the references are about icing conditions. If a pilot's practical test is in a simulator, there is a good possibility the examiner might have the weather below freezing. This would be so the examiner can complete objective 2 about the knowledge part. If in the aircraft the examiner may simulate freezing conditions to determine a pilots level of knowledge.

> "Spectacular achievement is always
> preceded by unspectacular preparation."
> **-ROBERT H. SCHULLER**

TASK F: POWERPLANT FAILURE DURING TAKEOFF

NOTE: In a multiengine airplane certificated under 14 CFR parts 23 Commuter category, SFAR 41C 4(b), and part 25, with published V1, VR, and/or V2 speeds, the failure of the most critical powerplant should be simulated at a point:

1) after V1 and prior to V2, if in the opinion of the examiner, it is appropriate under the prevailing conditions; or

2) as close as possible after V1 when V1 and V2 or V1 and VR are identical.

In a multiengine airplane certificated under 14 CFR part 23 (except commuter category), (for which no V1, VR, or V2 speeds are published) the failure of the most critical powerplant should be simulated at a point after reaching a minimum of VSSE and, if accomplished in the aircraft, at an altitude not lower than 400 feet AGL, giving consideration to local atmospheric conditions, terrain, and aircraft performance available.

In a simulator, there are no limitations on powerplant failures in either airplane by certification basis.

APPLICANT NOTE: Expect this task to be combined with normal Task A, and/or Task E at examiner's discretion.

References

- Part 61- 61.157 areas of operation

- POH/AFM

- FAA-H-8083-3 - Airplane Flying Handbook

- FSB Report

Objective: To determine that the applicant:

1. Exhibits satisfactory knowledge of the procedures used during powerplant failure on takeoff, the appropriate reference airspeeds, and the specific pilot actions required.

2. Takes into account, prior to beginning the takeoff, operational factors which could affect the maneuver, such as Takeoff Warning Inhibit Systems or other airplane characteristics, runway length, surface conditions, wind, wake turbulence, visibility, precipitation, obstructions, and other related factors that could adversely affect safety.

3. Completes required checks prior to starting takeoff to verify the expected powerplant performance. Performs all required pre-takeoff checks as required by the appropriate checklist items or coordinates with crew to ensure completion of checklist items in a timely manner and as recommended by the manufacturer.

4. Aligns the airplane on the runway/waterway.

5. Applies the controls correctly to maintain longitudinal alignment on the centerline of the runway, if appropriate, prior to initiating and during the takeoff.

6. Adjusts the powerplant controls as recommended by the FAA-approved guidance for the existing conditions.

7. Single-engine airplanes - establishes a power-off descent approximately straight-ahead, if the powerplant failure occurs after becoming airborne and before reaching an altitude where a safe turn can be made.

8. Continues the takeoff (in a 14 CFR part 25 or 14 CFR section 23.3(d) commuter multiengine airplane) if the (simulated) powerplant failure occurs at a point where the airplane can continue to a specified airspeed and altitude at the end of the runway commensurate with the airplane's performance capabilities and operating limitations.

9. Maintains (in a multiengine airplane), after a simulated powerplant failure and after a climb has been established, the desired heading within ±5°, desired airspeed within ±5 knots, and, if appropriate for the airplane, establishes a bank of approximately 5°, or as recommended by the manufacturer, toward the operating powerplant.

10. Maintains the airplane alignment with the heading appropriate for climb performance and terrain clearance when powerplant failure occurs.

11. Acknowledges and makes appropriate callouts to crew, if in crew served aircraft.

Explained

Really focus on maintaining very good airspeed and heading control. Understand the appropriate engine failure during takeoff continued profile. In a crew environment ensure that the pilot monitoring understands exactly what should be done. Establish very good CRM.

Usually the best performances I see is when the PF realizes their number one focus is to fly the aircraft and put the PM to work. The bottom line is establish standard procedures for the PF and PM and use good CRM. Usually the PF performance is poor because the pilot is trying to do too many other tasks when the pilot should be flying the aircraft. If a pilot is single pilot, flying the aircraft is still number one while dividing attention only to do necessary tasks like verifying the propeller feathered, etc.

The applicant note under this task indicates this task can be combined with Task A and/or E of this section. This is the normal/crosswind takeoff and the instrument takeoff. The normal/crosswind takeoff is a VMC maneuver so the powerplant failure during takeoff can be VMC initially but I would expect the examiner to simulate IMC soon after takeoff.

"The best preparation for tomorrow
is doing your best today."
-H. JACKSON BROWN, JR.

TASK G: REJECTED TAKEOFF

References

- Part 61- 61.157 areas of operation

- POH/AFM

- FAA-H-8083-3 - Airplane Flying Handbook

- AC 120-62 - Takeoff Safety Training Aid (12 pages) (this AC announces the availability of a more in-depth takeoff safety training aid. The actual training aid is 298 pages.

Objective: To determine that the applicant understands when to reject or continue the takeoff and:

1. Exhibits satisfactory knowledge of the technique and procedure for accomplishing a rejected takeoff after powerplant/system(s) failure/warnings, including related safety factors.

2. Takes into account, prior to beginning the takeoff, operational factors, which could affect the maneuver, such as Takeoff

Warning Inhibit Systems or other airplane characteristics, runway length, surface conditions, wind, visibility, precipitation, obstructions, and aircraft cleared for LAHSO that could affect takeoff performance and could adversely affect safety.

3. Aligns the airplane on the runway centerline or clear of obstacles and vessels on waterways.

4. Performs all required pre-takeoff checks as required by the appropriate checklist items or coordinates with crew to ensure completion of checklist items in a timely manner and as recommended by the manufacturer.

5. Adjusts the powerplant controls as recommended by the FAA approved guidance for the existing conditions.

6. Applies the controls correctly to maintain longitudinal alignment on the centerline of the runway.

7. Aborts the takeoff if, in a single-engine airplane the powerplant failure occurs prior to becoming airborne, or in a multiengine airplane, the powerplant failure occurs at a point during the takeoff where the abort procedure can be initiated and the airplane can be safely stopped on the remaining runway/ stopway. If a flight simulator is not used, the powerplant failure must be simulated before reaching 50 percent of VMC.

8. Reduces the power smoothly and promptly, if appropriate to the airplane, when powerplant failure is recognized.

9. Uses spoilers, prop reverse, thrust reverse, wheel brakes, and other drag/braking devices, as appropriate, maintaining positive control in such a manner as to bring the airplane to a safe stop.

10. Accomplishes the appropriate powerplant failure or other procedures and/or checklists or coordinates with crew to ensure completion of checklist items in a timely manner and as recommended by the manufacturer, as set forth in the POH or AFM.

Explained

Call for the appropriate checklist and notify ATC. This is often missed or not accomplished very well. A good technique is to state the runway the aircraft is on when notifying ATC. "Atlanta tower, N123AB is aborting the takeoff on runway 26L due to an engine failure."

Notice objective 7 indicates an engine failure. The rejected takeoff task has to be completed using an engine failure or else this objective is not completed and therefore the task is not completed.

> "One of life's most painful moments comes when we must admit that we didn't do our homework, that we are not prepared."
> **–MERLIN OLSEN**

TASK H: DEPARTURE PROCEDURES

References

- Part 61- 61.157 areas of operation

- POH/AFM

- AIM

- AC 90-100 - U.S. Terminal and En Route Area Navigation (RNAV) Operations (29 pages)

- FAA-H-8261-1 - Instrument Procedures Handbook

- FAA-H-8083-15 - Instrument Flying Handbook

Objective: To determine that the applicant:

1. In actual or simulated instrument conditions, exhibits satisfactory knowledge of DPs, En Route Low and High Altitude Charts, FMSP, and related pilot/controller responsibilities.

2. Uses the current and appropriate navigation publications for the proposed flight.

3. Selects, configures, and uses the appropriate communications frequencies, navigation and systems displays; selects and identifies the navigation aids and routes necessary to properly fly the assigned ATC clearance.

4. Coordinates with crew in crew served aircraft to ensure performance of, or performs the appropriate checklist items in a timely manner and as recommended by the manufacturer.

5. Establishes communications with ATC, using proper phraseology and advises ATC when unable to comply with a clearance or restriction.

6. Complies, in a timely manner, with all instructions and airspace restrictions.

7. Exhibits adequate knowledge of two-way radio communications failure procedures.

8. Intercepts, in a timely manner, all courses, radials, and bearings appropriate to the procedure, route, clearance, or as directed by the examiner.

9. Maintains the appropriate airspeed within ±10 knots, headings within ±10°, altitude within ±100 feet; and accurately tracks a course, radial, or bearing.

10. Conducts the departure phase to a point where, in the opinion of the examiner, the transition to the en route environment is complete.

Explained

There is a lot of information provided in the resources listed under this task. Based on what I've seen in training pilots, most pilots need to spend a good bit of time reviewing this particular subject, departure procedures. Study each resource and focus on the information related to departure procedures.

If the aircraft is equipped with a FMS, the examiner needs to evaluate the pilot on this subject. Be prepared, there is a lot of information the examiner can cover with different types of scenarios. For example, how would you using the FMS if the GPS was inoperative?

Be able to answer questions like these:

- What performance criteria am I required to meet during a departure procedure?
- How is a climb gradient calculated?
- What performance will the aircraft have if the aircraft experiences an engine failure (multiengine)?
- Is a pilot required by the regulations to meet a departure procedure with single engine performance?

Many questions about this should be asked during the task Performance and Limitations. If a pilot is not demonstrating knowledge during the practical test, the examiner can ask questions.

This subject has a lot of possible questions. Pilots should take their time and be prepared.

Have current charts.

Expect the examiner to simulate communication failure to test a pilots knowledge about two-way radio communications failure procedures as indicated in objective 7.

The GPS receiver must be set to terminal (±1 NM) CDI sensitivity and the navigation routes contained in the database in order to fly published IFR charted departures and DPs.

Backup

Some pilots like to backup the FMS or GPS during a departure procedure. Use the avionics provided to the fullest extent, but it is not required. Active monitoring of alternative navigation equipment is not required if the GPS receiver uses RAIM for integrity monitoring. Active monitoring of an alternate means of navigation is required when the RAIM capability of the GPS equipment is lost. Procedures must be established for use in the event that the loss of RAIM capability is predicted to occur. In situations where this is encountered, the flight must rely on other approved equipment, delay departure, or cancel the flight.1

Crosscheck

Flight crews should crosscheck the cleared flight plan against charts or other applicable resources, as well as the navigation system textual display and the aircraft map display, if applicable. If required, confirm exclusion of a specific navigation aid. A procedure should not be used if doubt exists as to the validity of the procedure in the navigation database.

When it comes to the simulator, I see pilots get very sloppy when it comes to verifying their route. Play the game and do as you would in the aircraft.

Verification of assigned route and correct entry of transitions into RNAV System/ Flight Management System (FMS). 2

DPs. Prior to flight, pilots must verify their aircraft navigation system is operating correctly and the correct runway and departure procedure (including any applicable en route transition) are entered and properly depicted. Pilots who are assigned an RNAV departure procedure and subsequently receive a change of runway, procedure or transition must verify the appropriate changes are entered and available for navigation prior to takeoff. A final check of proper runway entry and correct route depiction, shortly before takeoff, is recommended. 1

Routes. Pilots must verify proper entry of their ATC assigned route upon initial clearance and any subsequent change of route. Pilots must ensure the waypoints sequence depicted by their navigation system matches the route depicted on the appropriate chart(s) and their assigned route. 2

STARs. Pilots must verify their aircraft navigation system is operating correctly and the correct arrival procedure and runway (including any applicable transition) are entered and properly depicted. 2

Map Displays

Use of navigation map displays. Prior to takeoff, pilots of aircraft with a navigation map display should verify the relationship of the aircraft position symbol to their assigned runway (if available) and route on their display matches external visual cues, as well as charts. Specifically, once on or near their assigned runway, pilots should ensure their navigation display reflects the same relative position to the runway and the route depiction reflects that of the respective chart. During flight, these displays should be used in concert with textual displays for route verification. 2

Lateral Deviation Indicator

Pilots must use a lateral deviation indicator (or equivalent navigation map display), flight director and/or autopilot in lateral navigation mode on RNAV 1 routes. Pilots are encouraged to use a lateral deviation indicator (or equivalent navigation map display), flight director and/or autopilot in lateral navigation mode on RNAV 2 routes. 2

I see some pilots that have come from environments like the military where hand flying is heavily emphasized. In most civilian operations good automation management is emphasized. Follow the guidance in the AIM and use the autopilot. Some RNAV departure procedures will indicate the autopilot is to be used.

> "I've always considered myself to be just average talent and what I have is a ridiculous insane obsessiveness for practice and preparation."
> **–WILL SMITH**

IV. Inflight Maneuvers

TASK A: STEEP TURNS

References

- Part 61- 61.157 areas of operation

- FAA-H-8083-3 - Airplane Flying Handbook

- POH/AFM

- FSB Report

Objective: To determine that the applicant:

1. In actual or simulated instrument conditions, exhibits knowledge of steep turns (if applicable to the airplane) and the factors associated with performance; and, if applicable, wing loading, angle of bank, stall speed, pitch, power requirements, and over-banking tendencies.

2. Selects an altitude recommended by the manufacturer, training syllabus, or other training directive, but in no case lower than 3,000 feet AGL.

3. Establishes the recommended entry airspeed.

4. Rolls into a coordinated turn of 180° or 360° with a bank of at least 45°. Maintains the bank angle within ±5° while in smooth, stabilized flight.

5. Applies smooth coordinated pitch, bank, and power to maintain the specified altitude within ±100 feet and the desired airspeed within ±10 knots.

6. Rolls out of the turn (at approximately the same rate as used to roll into the turn) within ±10° of the entry or specified heading, stabilizes the airplane in a straight-and-level attitude or, at the discretion of the examiner, reverses the direction of turn and repeats the maneuver in the opposite direction.

7. Avoids any indication of an approaching stall, abnormal flight attitude, or exceeding any structural or operating limitation during any part of the maneuver.

Explained

When practicing steep turns determine the exact pitch attitude and power setting that will maintain the target airspeed. The aircraft POH probably does not provide information on conducting steep turns. The FSB report may if there is a FSB report. The airspeed that is chosen should be below maneuvering speed (Va). Objective 3 of this task indicates to establish the recommended entry airspeed. The instructor should provide guidance in selecting the proper entry airspeed.

Be sure to check for a FSB Report.

"But to me the bottom line is the more education you can give yourself, and the more preparation you can do, the less chance of failing."

–STUART PEARCE

TASK B: APPROACHES TO STALLS AND STALL RECOVERY

References

- Part 61- 61.157 areas of operation

- FAA-H-8083-3 - Airplane Flying Handbook

- POH/AFM

- FSB Report

Three approaches to stall are required, as follows (unless otherwise specified by the FSB Report):

1. One in the takeoff configuration (except where the airplane uses only zero-flap takeoff configuration) or approach (partial) flap configuration.

2. One in a clean cruise configuration.

3. One in a landing configuration (landing gear and landing flaps set).

CAUTION: Avoid deep stalls which are termed as "virtually unrecoverable" in airplanes, and "tip stalls" in swept wing airplanes.

One of these approaches to a stall must be accomplished while in a turn using a bank angle of 15 to 30°.

NOTE: When published, the aircraft manufacturer's procedures for the specific make/model/series airplane take precedent over the identification and recovery actions herein. One of these approaches to a stall must be accomplished while in a turn with a bank angle of 15 to 30. If installed, one of these approaches to a stall should be accomplished by commands to the autopilot.

Objective: To determine that the applicant:

1. In actual or simulated instrument conditions exhibits satisfactory knowledge of the factors, which influence stall characteristics, including the use of various drag configurations, power settings, pitch attitudes, weights, and bank angles. Also, demonstrates adequate knowledge of and skill in the proper procedure for resuming normal flight.

2. If accomplished in an airplane, selects an entry altitude that is in accordance with the AFM or POH, but in no case lower than an altitude that will allow recovery to be safely completed at a minimum of 3,000 feet AGL for non-transport certificated airplanes and 5,000 feet for transport certificated airplanes. When accomplished in an FSTD, the entry should be consistent with expected operational environment for the stall configuration with no minimum entry altitude defined.

3. Observes the area is clear of other aircraft prior to accomplishing an approach to a stall.

4. While maintaining the briefed profile, either manually or with the autopilot engaged, smoothly adjust pitch attitude, bank angle, and/or power setting that will induce a stall.

5. Announces the first indication of an impending stall (such as buffeting, stick shaker, decay of control effectiveness, and any other cues related to the specific airplane design characteristics) and promptly initiates recovery by disconnecting autopilot, reducing the angle of attack, leveling the wings, increasing power as necessary, and retracting any speedbrakes/spoilers to effect a safe and timely recovery.

    Note: If accomplished in an airplane in actual flight, the power should be set in accordance with the evaluator's instructors, when a limitation of power application is prudent for operational considerations and safety is not impaired.

6. Regains control of the airplane and **recovers to maneuvering speed** and flight path appropriate for the airplane's configuration without exceeding the airplane's limitations or losing excessive altitude consistent with the airplane's performance capabilities. This should include reducing pitch attitude as necessary, reducing bank angle and adding power (no particular order implied!) to recover to missed approach or cruise configuration, airspeed and altitude. Some altitude loss is expected during the recovery, but re-establishment of controlled flight is paramount.

    Note: Evaluation criteria for a recovery from an approach to stall should not mandate a predetermined value for altitude loss and should not mandate maintaining altitude during recovery. Valid evaluation criteria must take into account the multitude of external (such as density altitude) and internal variables (ie. airplane mass, drag configuration and powerplant response time) which affect the recovery altitude.

7. Demonstrates smooth, positive control during entry, approach to a stall, and recovery.

Explained

A FSB report can change how the pilot conducts the stalls during the practical test. For example the Citation 560XL has a FSB report that has a recommended procedure for stall recovery. The examiner should be familiar with the FSB report if there is one, and the pilot should follow the FSB report recommendation.

142 training centers are required to have specific profiles located in the information provided to the pilot during training. Flight schools will probably provide stall profiles. Many schools will provide stall profile information and guidance. Is the pilot required to follow the stall profiles on the practical test? I would say the pilot is not required because it is not part of the references listed above. Also, the examiner is acting as a representative of the FAA and the examiner is to evaluate the pilot based on the PTS and the references listed under this task. More than likely a pilot will perform the maneuver as trained, but as long as the pilot understands what is controlling for the task stalls. The examiner can ask a pilot to perform the task a certain way.

Due to safety in the aircraft there is not much freedom but in a simulator there is a lot of freedom. Objective 2 indicates the stalls should be conducted as they would actually happen. A landing stall should be accomplished on landing, not at altitude as a maneuver.

Objective 3 requires the pilot to verify the area is clear of other aircraft. In a simulator this objective really is useless and the way I view it, if the examiner clears the pilot for a stall maneuver, the area is assumed to be clear of other aircraft. Play the game if needed. Obviously in the actual aircraft this is a very important objective. Ask how to handle this objective during the brief before the flight portion of the practical test in a simulator.

Notice that objective 5 requires that the pilot to announce the first indication of an impending stall.

Notice that a decay in control effectiveness is also a first indication of an impending stall.

Objective 5 does indicate that the examiner can specify what power setting to use during the recovery. If the examiner does not provide direction, then maximum power is required.

What is a pilot is truly being evaluated on during a stall maneuver? It is that the pilot recognizes the first indication of an impending stall, recovers to a reference airspeed, altitude and heading with minimal loss of altitude, airspeed, and heading deviation. Demonstrates smooth, positive control during entry, approach to a stall, and recovery. Notice it does not indicate the pilot needs to have any type of maneuver memorized. It helps the instructor, examiner and you if you do know how to do the three stall maneuvers.

Notice also there is no limitation on autopilot use. Use the autopilot to your advantage and for each maneuver configure the aircraft while the autopilot remains engaged and then turn it off. Obviously the recovery has to be hand flown. Entering the stall with the autopilot on is an option which is the most realistic situation. The PTS now indicates at least one stall should be entered with the autopilot.

There is a movement towards scenario-based training. In the simulator I think a stall is best performed simulating the actual condition of flight. For example, the landing stall should be performed on final approach to landing. A departure stall should be performed during the departure phase of flight. A simulator allows the freedom to do this and I think pilots receive better training when the stalls are conducted in this manner. There is nothing in the PTS requiring a stall to be performed as a maneuver at altitude in a simulator. If a pilot wanted to be trained by doing the stalls consistent with expected operational environment for the stall configurations, the pilot should be allowed to do this. In fact objective 2 under the task approach to stalls it states "When accomplished in an FTD or flight simulator, the entry altitude should be consistent with expected operational environment for the stall configuration." I read this statement to indicate if the training is in a simulator, the typical stall maneuver should not be conducted. The stall should be simulated as real as possible. For example a departure stall should be conducted during the departure phase of flight. Talk with your flight instructor and your examiner to come up with a plan.

Objective 6 explains a lot about what is expected of the pilot.

Positive Rate

One discussion I have had a lot with pilots is about a positive rate of indication during a stall recovery and when to raise the landing gear. Let's look at an example, what if during a practical test the examiner stated that during the approach to landing stall the pilot must not raise the landing gear without a positive rate during a stall recovery. Now positive rate makes sense if the aircraft was close to the runway and there was a possibility of a touch down. If there is no FSB report discussing positive rate, or no profile or procedure in the POH/AFM for approach and landing stall and/or the POH/AFM does not require the pilot to have a positive rate, can the examiner require this?

The only reference listed under the task stalls that contains profile information is FAA-H-8083-3, Airplane Flying Handbook. This book does indicate a positive rate is when to retract the landing gear on power off stalls and power on stalls. I'm not saying I disagree with a positive rate, but what if the pilot indicates the aircraft was at a safe altitude and they were more concerned with reducing drag and the landing gear being down provided no benefit at the higher altitude. I believe there is a point to be made here. With the Airplane Flying Handbook being the only reference indicating a positive rate the examiner can reference this information to support a positive rate. But if the pilot's response was that they felt the aircraft was at a safe altitude and a positive rate was not necessary and that the maneuver was never seriously in doubt, I see it as being very hard for an examiner to fail a pilot for this reason. Especially when a positive rate is not required in any of the objectives under the task stalls in the PTS and is probably not required in the POH/AFM.

Interesting fact is that the Private PTS and the Commercial PTS indicate a positive rate is required for retracting the landing gear during a stall recovery.

The reason I am bringing this up is because I have heard examiners indicate they would fail a pilot if the landing gear was retracted during a stall recovery without a positive rate. If I were the pilot taking the practical test I would have to disagree. Especially if the outcome of the maneuver was never in doubt, I was very aware of the situation, the POH/AFM provides no guidance on stall recovery and the FSB report, if there is one does not address a positive rate during stall recovery. This is one of those situations I have seen examiners add their own objective outside of the PTS and references.

What really is positive rate or positive climb? Using the King Air 350 POH as an example, positive climb is only associated with take off and the balk landing. Positive rate is only associated with the ground proximity warning system. Positive climb is obviously important when the aircraft is taking off because it means it is leaving the ground. The definition of a balk landing is a go around being initiated at 50 feet above the runway. Positive rate and positive climb make sense here. But during a stall recovery positive rate does not make sense if the pilot has good situational awareness and determines touchdown is not a factor and reducing drag and resuming normal flight is more important to safety.

Configuration Change

The stall task under objective 1 indicates the pilot should exhibit adequate knowledge of the proper procedure for resuming normal flight. What if the POH/AFM does not provide a profile for the proper procedure for resuming normal flight after a stall? Let me give an example using the King Air 350. The profile for the landing stall provided by some training centers and used by many King Air pilots is the same as the balk landing procedure that is provided in the checklist of the POH. Should the pilot be required to use this procedure for resuming normal flight?

Balk Landing Checklist: (BE-350 POH)

1. Power . . . . MAXIMUM ALLOWABLE

2. Airspeed . . . . MAINTAIN VREF
(when clear of obstacles, establish a normal climb)

3. Flaps (at VREF + 10 knots) . . . . APPROACH

4. Landing Gear (when a positive climb is established). . . . . UP

5. Flaps (at 125 knots, minimum) . . . . UP

The stall recovery profile used by many training facilities is the same as above. There is nothing in the King Air POH that indicates a landing stall recovery should be conducted in the same manner.

I started to think about what should a pilot be expected to use as a stall configuration change during recover. For most airplanes the only reference under this task that provides even a little bit of guidance is the Airplane Flying Handbook. I provided some of the information about configuration change and resuming normal flight below.

Airplane Flying Handbook:

Recovering from the stall should be accomplished by reducing the angle of attack, releasing back-elevator pressure, and advancing the throttle to maximum allowable power.

Power off stall, when stall occurs, reduce angle of attack and add full power. Raise flaps as recommended (this may not be recommended in the POH). After establishing a positive rate of climb, the flaps and landing gear are retracted, as necessary.

The Airplane Flying Handbook does provide some guidance on a positive rate and raising the gear. Again I ask, what if a pilot raised the landing gear during a landing stall without a positive rate and the pilot had sufficient altitude that a touchdown was not possible. Can the examiner fail the pilot for not resuming normal flight properly? As long as the maneuver was never seriously in doubt, I have to say no.

Notice the King Air 350 balk landing checklist also indicates the flaps should be retracted to approach at a speed of Vref+10. This is the profile used by training centers and King Air pilots for a landing stall recovery. Again, what if a pilot raised the flaps from full to approach at a speed less than Vref+10. Did the pilot fail the task? There is no guidance in the King Air POH. The airplane flying handbook does not provide much guidance. In fact the power off stall guidance in the Airplane Flying Handbook indicates raising the flaps after the angle of attack has been reduced. If an examiner did not agree with the King Air pilot retracting the flaps prior to Vref+10 and indicated the pilot failed the task, the pilot should ask the examiner, on what grounds is the pilot required to retract the flaps to approach at Vref+10. If the response is that is that the balk landing indicates this is the procedure, the pilot can say, I am doing a stall recovery, not a balk landing and where does it say I have to follow the balk landing procedure? If he indicates that it is the stall profile provided in the training materials, the pilot should ask, where does the PTS or the PTS references indicate I have to follow those profiles?

I hope this information is opening up your mind to understanding what is required of a pilot during the practical test. Pilots should understand this because I do know of pilots who have failed their practical tests without justification, but the pilots didn't know enough to provide a counter point of view. Pilots can always challenge an examiners decision.

During the takeoff configuration stall, if demonstrated with the landing gear in the extended position, then a positive rate makes sense and more than likely the POH/AFM indicates during the takeoff a positive rate is the point to retract the landing gear.

This is why it is important for the examiner to fully explain the scenario. If the examiner says the runway is at an elevation of 4000 feet in a particular stall scenario, and the aircraft is at 4200 feet during the approach to landing stall recovery, there probably is an argument for positive rate. But what if the aircraft is at 4800 feet and the examiner indicated the runway is at an elevation of 4000 feet. I would say as long as the pilot is in complete control the aircraft and the situation, and the pilot decides that reducing drag is more important, what objective did the pilot not comply with in the PTS under the task approach to stalls?

This is a very debatable area but I feel pilot should fully understand what is expected of them. If the pilot raises the landing gear without a positive rate look at the objectives under the approach to stall task and try to find an objective the pilot did not comply with? What information of the POH/AFM did the pilot not comply with? As an examiner it is very hard to support failing an applicant in this situation.

"Good luck is a residue of preparation."
—JACK YOUNGBLOOD

TASK C: POWERPLANT FAILURE - MULTIENGINE AIRPLANE

References

- Part 61- 61.157 areas of operation

- POH/AFM

Note: The feathering of one propeller and engine shutdown must be demonstrated in any multiengine airplane (or simulator/qualified FTD) equipped with propellers (includes turboprop), unless the airplane is an exception by the type rating and airplane certification (see page 13 of this document). The propeller must be safely feathered and unfeathered while airborne. In a multiengine jet airplane (or simulator/qualified FTD), one engine must be shut down and a restart must be demonstrated while airborne. Feathering or shutdown should be performed only under conditions and at such altitudes (no lower than 3,000 feet AGL) and in a position where a safe landing can be made on an established airport in the event difficulty is encountered in unfeathering the propeller or restarting the engine. At an altitude lower than 3,000 feet AGL, simulated engine failure will be performed by setting the powerplant controls to simulate zero-thrust. In the event the propeller cannot be unfeathered or the engine air started during the test, it should be treated as an emergency.

When authorized and conducted in a flight simulator, feathering or shutdown may be performed in conjunction with any procedure or maneuver and at locations and altitudes at the discretion of the examiner. However, when conducted in an FTD, authorizations are limited to shutdown, feathering, restart, and/or unfeathering procedures only. See appendix 1.

Objective: To determine that the applicant:

1. Exhibits knowledge of the flight characteristics and controllability associated with maneuvering with powerplant(s) inoperative (as appropriate to the airplane).

2. Maintains positive airplane control. Establishes a bank of approximately 5°, if required, or as recommended by the

manufacturer, to maintain coordinated flight, and properly trims for that condition.

3. Sets powerplant controls, reduces drag as necessary, correctly identifies and verifies the inoperative powerplant(s) after the failure (or simulated failure).

4. Maintains the operating powerplant(s) within acceptable operating limits.

5. Follows the prescribed airplane checklist or coordinates with crew to ensure completion of checklist items in a timely manner and as recommended by the manufacturer, and verifies the procedures for securing the inoperative powerplant(s).

6. Determines the cause for the powerplant(s) failure and if a restart is a viable option.

7. Maintains desired altitude within ±100 feet, when a constant altitude is specified and is within the capability of the airplane.

8. Maintains the desired airspeed within ±10 knots.

9. Maintains the desired heading within ±10° of the specified heading.

10. Demonstrates proper powerplant restart procedures (if appropriate) in accordance with FAA-approved procedure/ checklist or the manufacturer's recommended procedures and pertinent checklist items.

Explained

Remember accuracy is immensely more important than the speed the checklist is completed. I've seen many pilots feel rushed during a powerplant failure and make mistakes like shutting down the wrong engine, closing the wrong firewall shut-off valve, turning the wrong generator off, etc. A pilot should take their time and positively identify what he is doing. Verify important actions with the other crew member if one is available. If operating single pilot it is even more important that the pilot take his time to be 100% accurate in all actions. The PTS does indicate the completion of checklist items in a timely manner.

Timely manner is subjective where not being 100% accurate during a powerplant failure will lead to a failure of the practical test.

Another point to make is in a crew environment, divide the workload efficiently so that one pilot is still monitoring the aircraft and/or flying the aircraft. Let me give you an example with a crew of two pilots in a multiengine aircraft. During an engine failure if the pilot flying continues to fly the aircraft and initiate the immediate action items for an engine failure, the PF is doing the majority of the work. During this time the PM is doing nothing more than watching and communicating with ATC. Ask yourself how effective are either of the pilots monitoring the aircraft. I think a better situation is where the PF continues to fly and monitor the aircraft while calling for the PM to initiate the immediate action items of the checklist. The PF can confirm any critical actions, for example a firewall shutoff valve being closed. Even though the PF is not physically doing the action, the PF has to confirm the action therefore the PF is still in complete control of the situation as PIC. Some pilots seem to think if they are not physically manipulating the controls, they are not acting as PIC and this is incorrect.

"The best preparation for tomorrow is to do today's work superbly well."
-WILLIAM OSLER

TASK D: POWERPLANT FAILURE - SINGLE-ENGINE AIRPLANE

References

- Part 61- 61.157 areas of operation

- FAA-H-8083-3 - Airplane Flying Handbook

- POH/AFM

Note: No simulated powerplant failure will be given by the examiner in an airplane when an actual touchdown cannot be safely completed, should it become necessary.

Objective: To determine that the applicant:

1. Exhibits knowledge of the flight characteristics, approach and forced (emergency) landing procedures, and related procedures to use in the event of a powerplant failure (as appropriate to the airplane).

2. Maintains positive control throughout the maneuver.

3. Establishes and maintains the recommended best glide airspeed, ±5 knots, and configuration during a simulated powerplant failure.

4. Selects a suitable airport or landing area, which is within the performance capability of the airplane.

5. Establishes a proper flight pattern to the selected airport or landing area, taking into account altitude, wind, terrain, obstructions, and other pertinent operational factors.

6. Follows the emergency checklist items appropriate to the airplane to ensure completion of checklist items in a timely manner and as recommended by the manufacturer.

7. Determines the cause for the simulated powerplant failure (if altitude permits) and if a restart is a viable option.

8. Uses configuration devices, such as landing gear and flaps in a manner recommended by the manufacturer and/or approved by the FAA.

> "What I do is prepare myself until I know I can do what I have to do."
>
> **–JOE NAMATH**

TASK E: SPECIFIC FLIGHT CHARACTERISTICS

References

- Part 61- 61.157 areas of operation

- FSB Reports

- POH/AFM

Objective:. To determine that the applicant:

1. Exhibits satisfactory knowledge of specific flight characteristics appropriate to the specific airplane, as identified by FSB Reports, such as Dutch Rolls for certain aircraft.

2. Uses proper technique to enter into, operate within, and recover from specific flight situations.

Explained

Pilots should check for a FSB report on their specific aircraft. For example the Challenger 604 and 605 FSB report identifies the following special flight characteristics:

"Special emphasis during training should be placed in the area of roll control during multiple hydraulic system failure, crosswind landing and rollout, and zero-flap landing.

The FSB has determined that zero-flap approaches and landings to a full stop are required to be demonstrated by applicants seeking type certification in this aircraft. The aircraft's trailing edge flap extension is powered by the electrical system and there is no alternate means of flap operation in the case of electrical system failure. The aircraft has a relatively high approach and landing speed and has a tendency to "float" if normal landing flare technique is used. Thrust reverser deployment during a zero flap landing tends to cause the nose to pitch-up, requiring significant pilot input to maintain nose wheel contact with the runway."

Link: http://fsims.faa.gov/PICResults.aspx?mode=Publication&doc type=FSB%20Reports

> "A winning effort begins with preparation."
> **–JOE GIBBS**

TASK F: RECOVERY FROM UNUSUAL ATTITUDES

References

- Part 61- 61.157 areas of operation

- FSB Reports

- FAA-H-8083-15 - Instrument Flying Handbook

- POH/AFM

Objective: To determine that the applicant:

1. Exhibits knowledge of recovery from unusual attitudes.

2. Recovers from nose-high banked and/or level unusual attitudes, using proper pitch, bank, and power techniques.

3. Recovers from nose-low banked and/or level unusual attitudes, using proper pitch, bank, and power techniques.

Explained

Chapter 5 of the Instrument Flying Handbook provides information on unusual attitudes. The examiner's questions are to come from the PTS and the listed references, but remember there should be no questions if the pilot demonstrates the correct level of knowledge.

In the case of unusual attitudes the examiner is very limited because the aircraft POH/AFM typically does not have much information, if any at all. The instrument flying handbook has a small section devoted to unusual attitudes. For a better understanding of unusual attitudes the pilot will need to search other sources of information.

Remember earlier in the PTS under references it was stated "publications other than those listed may be used for references if their content conveys substantially the same meaning as the referenced publications." Would you consider a reference other than what is in the PTS that refers to recovery from unusual attitudes fair game?

For example, on www.faa.gov is a document titled Airplane Upset Recovery. Would it be fair for the examiner to ask a question from this document that is related to this task, but the answer cannot be found in the references list above. Like I indicated, there is not much in the Instrument Flying Handbook on unusual attitudes. Even though the Airplane Upset Recovery document is about unusual attitudes it is not a reference in this task.

Objective 1 indicates the pilot is to exhibit knowledge of the recovery from unusual attitudes. For example the Instrument Flying Handbook covers nose-low attitude recovery. If the pilot demonstrates a nose-low recovery as explained in the Instrument Flying Handbook, the objective is complete and no questions should be asked. If the examiner has to ask questions to verify knowledge he should expect answers that follow the guidance in the Instrument Flying Handbook. If the Airplane Upset Recovery document supports that information with the same meaning that is ok.

Couple of Examples:

During the oral exam the examiner asks "as a general rule how do you determine an unusual attitude is occurring?" An answer to this question can be found in the Instrument Flying Handbook. But this is not part of the oral exam which is the task Equipment Examination and Performance and Limitations. I would say this is not a valid question.

Ok, now during the flight or after the flight the examiner asks the same question to verify knowledge. Again I would say it is not a valid question because it does not fit under any of the objectives. Objective 1 is that the pilot exhibits knowledge of recovery from unusual attitudes and that is specific. An appropriate question would be about the recovery procedure if the pilot did not exhibit the knowledge by demonstration of the maneuver. If the pilot demonstrated an adequate level of knowledge about the recover from unusual attitudes, there should be no questions.

Summary

I expanded on this idea of what is a fair question and what is not. I think this same premise can be applied to any task.

"My own position is so far on the obsessive
side of preparation and professionalism
that I fear my point of view is not
going to be shared by anyone."

–JONNY WILKINSON

Note: There is a lot of truth to the above quote. I think if you prepare very well for your practical test you will be surprised how many pilots and examiners will not see your point of view. As I learned more and more about the requirements of the practical test, I started to see how different my point of view was from others. I wasn't just making things up, I could back up my point of view with published information.

V. Instrument Procedures

Note: TASKS B through F are not required if the applicant holds a private pilot or commercial pilot certificate and is seeking a type rating limited to VFR.

TASK A: STANDARD TERMINAL ARRIVAL/ FLIGHT MANAGEMENT SYSTEM PROCEDURES

References

- Part 61- 61.157 areas of operation

- POH/AFM

- AIM

- En Route Low and High Altitude Charts

- Profile Descent Charts

- STARs/FMSPs

- Standard Instrument Approach Procedure Charts (SIAP)

- FAA-H-8261-1 - Instrument Procedures Handbook

- AC 61-134 - General Aviation Controlled Flight Into Terrain Awareness (18 pages)

- AC 90-100 - U.S. Terminal and En Route Area Navigation (RNAV) Operations (29 pages)

Objective: To determine that the applicant:

1. In actual or simulated instrument conditions, exhibits adequate knowledge of En Route Low and High Altitude Charts, STARs/FMSPs, Instrument Approach Procedure Charts (IAP), and related pilot and controller responsibilities.

2. Uses the current and appropriate navigation publications for the proposed flight.

3. Selects and correctly identifies all instrument references, flight director and autopilot controls, displays, and navigation and communications equipment associated with the arrival.

4. Performs the airplane checklist items or coordinates with crew to ensure completion of checklist items appropriate to the arrival in a timely manner and as recommended by the manufacturer.

5. Establishes communications with ATC, using proper phraseology.

6. Complies, in a timely manner, with all ATC clearances, instructions, and restrictions. Advises ATC if unable to comply with ATC clearances or instructions.

7. Exhibits satisfactory knowledge of two-way communications failure procedures.

8. Intercepts, in a timely manner, all courses, radials, and bearings appropriate to the procedure, route, ATC clearance, or as directed by the examiner.

9. Adheres to airspeed restrictions and adjustments required by regulations, ATC, the POH, the AFM, or the examiner.

10. Establishes, where appropriate, a rate of descent consistent with the airplane operating characteristics and safety.

11. Maintains the appropriate airspeed/V-speed within ±10 knots, but not less than VREF, if applicable; heading ±10°; altitude within ±100 feet; and accurately tracks radials, courses, and bearings.

12. Complies with the provisions of the Profile Descent, STAR, and other arrival procedures, as appropriate.

Explained

Here again it is important to have current and all necessary charts.

Objective 12 talks about a profile descent. There is a movement towards Optimize Profile Descent's (ODP) on arrivals to airports where the aircraft can descend toward the runway more continuously, rather than having to maintain level flight during much of the approach, as they do now. There's a good chance during the practical test the pilot will not fly an arrival that has an ODP. But if flying a STAR and ATC gives a descend at pilots discretion, the best profile for this dissent is at least a 3° descent path.

Review descend via procedures in the AIM.

This is one of the few tasks that include the AIM as a reference. Pilots need to plan ahead and be prepared because of the amount of information.

Read the objectives of this task. The examiner must complete all tasks in the ATP PTS that apply to the pilot or aircraft. To complete this task the examiner must have the pilot fly a STAR. Plan on it and be prepared.

If the aircraft is equipped with a FMS or GPS, be able to program it correctly and use the available features.

"You had better live your best and act your best and think your best today; for today is the sure preparation for tomorrow and all the other tomorrows that follow."

–HARRIET MARTINEAU

TASK B: HOLDING

References

- Part 61- 61.157 areas of operation
- POH/AFM
- AIM
- En Route Low and High Altitude Charts
- Profile Descent Charts
- STARs
- Standard Instrument Approach Procedure Charts (SIAP)

Objective: To determine that the applicant:

1. In actual or simulated instrument conditions, exhibits knowledge of holding procedures for standard and nonstandard, published and non-published holding patterns. If appropriate, demonstrates satisfactory knowledge of holding endurance, including, but not necessarily limited to, fuel on board, fuel flow while holding, fuel required to alternate, etc.

2. Changes to the recommended holding airspeed appropriate for the airplane and holding altitude, so as to cross the holding fix at or below maximum holding airspeed.

3. Recognizes arrival at the clearance limit or holding fix.

4. Follows appropriate entry procedures for a standard, nonstandard, published, or non-published holding pattern.

5. Complies with ATC reporting requirements.

6. Uses the proper timing criteria required by the holding altitude and ATC or examiner's instructions.

7. Complies with the holding pattern leg length when a distance measuring equipment (DME) distance is specified.

8. Uses the proper wind-drift correction techniques to accurately maintain the desired radial, track, courses, or bearing.

9. Arrives over the holding fix as close as possible to the "expect further clearance" time.

10. Maintains the appropriate airspeed/V-speed within ±10 knots, altitude within ±100 feet, headings within ±10°; and accurately tracks radials, courses, and bearings.

11. Selects and correctly identifies required instrument navigation aids, flight director and autopilot controls, navigation equipment displays associated with the holding clearance and expected clearance, as appropriate.

Explained

If the aircraft is FMS equipped be prepared to use it for fuel planning questions. Objective 1 can require the pilot to demonstrate satisfactory knowledge of holding endurance and fuel planning. Be able to locate any performance charts related to holding.

To complete objective 1, the examiner should request the pilot to hold in a standard and nonstandard holding pattern. The examiner should also have the pilot demonstrate their skill by holding at a nonpublished holding pattern. Since the missed approach procedure task will usually have a standard or nonstandard holding pattern, there will be a requirement for the examiner to evaluate the other two holding requirements. To meet the other two requirements, the examiner can have the pilot execute an unpublished holding pattern that is opposite of the missed approach procedure holding pattern.

> "You hit home runs not by chance
> but by preparation."
> **–ROGER MARIS**

TASK C: PRECISION APPROACHES (PA)

References

- Part 61- 61.157 areas of operation

- POH/AFM

- AIM

- Standard Instrument Approach Procedure Charts (SIAP)

- FAA-H-8261-1 - Instrument Procedures Handbook

- FAA-H-8083-15 - Instrument Flying Handbook

Note: Two precision approaches, utilizing NAVAID equipment for centerline and glideslope guidance, must be accomplished in simulated or actual instrument conditions to DA/DH. At least one approach must be flown manually without the use of an autopilot. The second approach may be flown via the autopilot, if appropriate, and if the DA/DH altitude does not violate the authorized minimum altitude for autopilot operation. Manually flown precision approaches may use raw data displays or may be flight director assisted, at the discretion of the examiner.

If the aircraft is equipped with advanced flight instrument displays, the raw data approach should be flown by reference to the backup instrumentation as much as is possible with the airplane's configuration.

For multiengine airplanes at least one manually controlled precision approach must be accomplished with a simulated failure of one powerplant. The simulated powerplant failure should occur before initiating the final approach segment and must continue to touchdown or throughout the missed approach procedure. As the markings on localizer/glideslope indicators vary, a one-quarter scale deflection of either the localizer, or glide slope indicator is when it is displaced one-fourth of the distance that it may be deflected from the on glide slope or on localizer position.

Note: A stabilized approach is characterized by a constant angle, constant rate of descent approach profile ending near the touchdown point, where the landing maneuver begins.

Note: If the installed equipment and data base is current and qualified for IFR flight and LPV approaches, an LPV approach can be flown to demonstrate precision approach proficiency if the LPV DA is equal to or less than 300 feet HAT."

Objective: To determine that the applicant:

1. Exhibits satisfactory knowledge of the precision instrument approach procedures with all engines operating, and with one engine inoperative.

2. Accomplishes the appropriate precision instrument approaches as selected by the examiner.

3. Establishes two-way communications with ATC using the proper communications phraseology and techniques, or, directs co-pilot/safety pilot to do so, as appropriate for the phase of flight or approach segment.

4. Complies, in a timely manner, with all clearances, instructions, and procedures.

5. Advises ATC anytime the applicant is unable to comply with a clearance.

6. Establishes the appropriate airplane configuration and airspeed/V-speed considering turbulence, wind shear, microburst conditions, or other meteorological and operating conditions.

7. Completes the airplane checklist items or coordinates with crew to ensure completion of checklist items in a timely manner and as recommended by the manufacturer, appropriate to the phase of flight or approach segment, including engine out approach and landing checklists, if appropriate.

8. Prior to beginning the final approach segment, maintains the desired altitude ±100 feet, the desired airspeed within ±10 knots, the desired heading within ±5°; and accurately tracks radials, courses, and bearings.

9. Selects, tunes, identifies, and monitors the operational status of ground and airplane navigation equipment used for the approach, or correctly programs and monitors the RNAV equipment to display the proper course/track.

10. Applies the necessary adjustments to the published DA/DH and visibility criteria for the airplane approach category as required, such as -

    a. Notices to Airmen, including Flight Data Center (FDC) Procedural NOTAMs.

    b. Inoperative airplane and ground navigation equipment.

    c. Inoperative visual aids associated with the landing environment.

    d. National Weather Service (NWS) reporting factors and criteria.

11. Establishes a predetermined rate of descent at the point where the electronic glideslope begins, which approximates that required for the airplane to follow the glideslope.

12. Maintains a stabilized final approach, from the precision final approach fix to DA/DH, allowing no more than one-quarter scale deflection of either the glideslope or localizer indications, and maintains the desired airspeed within ±5 knots.

13. A missed approach or transition to a landing must be initiated at DA/DH.

14. Immediately initiates and executes the missed approach when at the DA/DH, if the required visual references for the runway Transitions to a normal landing approach (missed approach for seaplanes) only when the airplane is in a position from which a descent to a landing on the runway can be made at a normal rate of descent using normal maneuvering.

16. Maintains localizer and glide slope within one-quarter-scale deflection of the indicators during the visual descent from

DA/DH to a point over the runway where the glideslope must be abandoned to accomplish a normal landing.

Explained

Often to meet this task an examiner will select two ILS approaches that are with an engine failure and one of those approaches hand flow. The engine out hand flown approach can be to a landing or a missed approach procedure. This will cover the ILS approach requirements and the engine out ILS and engine out missed approach procedure. It can depend on the type of scenario the examiner is using. Don't be surprised if there are more approaches.

Pay attention to any NOTAMs or if the examiner simulates that some equipment is inoperative because objective 10 requires the pilot to apply the necessary adjustments.

Pilots are allowed only one quarter scale deflection of the glideslope or localizer so make sure during training that this is easily achievable.

Understand what visual references allow descent below DA/DH.

Objective 15 requires a pilot to use a normal rate of descent and normal maneuvering during the transition to a landing. During training make sure that the transition to landing is smooth. A pilot should not have a problem transitioning and crossing the threshold crossing height on target.

Objective 16 should not be in the task because it is not supported.

Note that objective 16 requires the pilot to maintain the localizer and glide slope within one-quarter-scale deflection of the indicators during the visual descent from DA/DH to a point over the runway where the glideslope must be abandoned to accomplish a normal landing. This objective should not be included in the list.

The AIM under 1–1–9 Instrument Landing System (ILS) has information contradicting objective 16. Under Glide Slope/Glide Path is the following:

The signal provides descent information for navigation down to the lowest authorized decision height (DH) specified in the approved ILS approach procedure. The glidepath may not be suitable for navigation below the lowest authorized DH and any reference to glidepath indications below that height must be supplemented by visual reference to the runway environment. Glidepaths with no published DH are usable to runway threshold.

The published glide slope threshold crossing height (TCH) DOES NOT represent the height of the actual glide path on–course indication above the runway threshold. It is used as a reference for planning purposes which represents the height above the runway threshold that an aircraft's glide slope antenna should be, if that aircraft remains on a trajectory formed by the four-mile-to-middle marker glidepath segment.

I think this is clear and a pilot should not reference the glide slope below DA.

"Luck, that's when preparation
and opportunity meet."

–PIERRE TRUDEAU

TASK D: NONPRECISION APPROACHES (NPA)

References

- Part 61- 61.157 areas of operation

- POH/AFM

- AIM

- Standard Instrument Approach Procedure Charts (SIAP)

- FAA-H-8261-1 -Instrument Procedures Handbook

- FAA-H-8083-15 - Instrument Flying Handbook

- AC 90-94 - Cancelled and replaced by AC 90-105, (39 pages)

Note: The applicant must accomplish at least two nonprecision approaches (one of which must include a procedure turn or, in the case of an RNAV approach, a Terminal Arrival Area (TAA) procedure) in simulated or actual weather conditions. At least one nonprecision approach must be flown without the use of autopilot and without the assistance of radar vectors. (The yaw damper and flight director are not considered parts of the autopilot for purpose of this part). The examiner will select nonprecision approaches that are representative of the type that the applicant is likely to use. The choices must utilize two different types of navigational aids. Some examples of navigational aids for the purpose of this part are: NDB, VOR, LOC, LDA, GPS, or RNAV.

Note: One approach should be flown with reference to backup or "fail down" instrumentation or navigation display depending on the aircraft's avionics configuration.

Note: The requirements for conducting a GPS approach for the purpose of this test are explained on pages 13 and 14 of the Introduction.

Objective: To determine that the applicant:

1. Exhibits adequate knowledge of nonprecision approach procedures representative of those the applicant is likely to use.

2. Accomplishes the nonprecision instrument approaches selected by the examiner.

3. Establishes two-way communications with ATC as appropriate to the phase of flight or approach segment and uses proper communications phraseology and techniques.

4. Complies with all clearances issued by ATC.

5. Advises ATC or the examiner any time the applicant is unable to comply with a clearance.

6. Establishes the appropriate airplane configuration and airspeed, and completes all applicable checklist items or coordinates with crew to ensure completion of checklist items in a timely manner and as recommended by the manufacturer.

7. Maintains, prior to beginning the final approach segment, the desired altitude ±100 feet, the desired airspeed ±10 knots, the desired heading ±5°; and accurately tracks radials, courses, and bearings.

8. Selects, tunes, identifies, and monitors the operational status of ground and airplane navigation equipment used for the approach.

9. Applies the necessary adjustments to the published Minimum Descent Altitude (MDA) and visibility criteria for the airplane approach category when required, such as -

   a. Notices to Airmen, including Flight Data Center Procedural NOTAMs.

   b. Inoperative airplane and ground navigation equipment.

   c. Inoperative visual aids associated with the landing environment.

   d. National Weather Service (NWS) reporting factors and criteria.

10. Establishes a rate of descent that will ensure arrival at the MDA (at, or prior to reaching, the visual descent point (VDP),

if published) with the airplane in a position from which a descent from MDA to a landing on the intended runway can be made at a normal rate using normal maneuvering.

11. Allows, while on the final approach segment, not more than quarter-scale deflection of the Course Deviation Indicator (CDI) or ±5° in the case of the RMI or bearing pointer, and maintains airspeed within ±5 knots of that desired.

12. Maintains the MDA, when reached, within −0, +50 feet to the missed approach point.

13. Executes the missed approach at the missed approach point if the required visual references for the intended runway are not unmistakably visible and identifiable at the missed approach point.

14. Executes a normal landing from a straight-in or circling approach when instructed by the examiner.

Explained

AC 90-94 was canceled January 23, 2009 and replaced by Approval Guidance for RNP Operations and Barometric Vertical Navigation in the U.S. National Airspace System.

During the practical test the pilot will be required to accomplish two non-precision approaches. Be prepared for a procedure turn or a Terminal Arrival Area (TAA) procedure in the case of an RNAV approach. If the aircraft has a FMS installed be sure to understand how to load the procedure turn or a transition.

VNAV

If the aircraft is equipped with approved VNAV capability the FAA is encouraging pilots to use this instead of the dive and drive method on RNAV approaches. If the aircraft has this capability, the pilot can use VNAV as advisory to a MDA. VNAV is strictly advisory when descending to a MDA and pilots should ensure the VNAV crosses all altitudes on the approach at the correct altitude. If the aircraft is authorized for LNAV/VNAV approaches, the pilot must follow the VNAV and in this case the aircraft is going to a decision altitude just like an ILS.

How does a pilot know the aircraft has Barometric VNAV Capability? According to AC90-105 Eligible aircraft are those with an Aircraft Flight Manual (AFM) or AFM Supplement which explicitly states that the VNAV system is approved for approach operations in accordance with AC 20-129 or AC 20-138. Located in the AIM under LNAV/VNAV approaches, it states:

> "this minima line can be flown by aircraft with a statement in the Aircraft Flight Manual that the installed equipment supports GPS approaches and has an approach-approved barometric VNAV, or if the aircraft has been demonstrated to support LNAV/VNAV approaches."

Basically, a pilot needs to refer to the POH.

LNAV/VNAV approaches are non-precision approaches. Even though these approaches use a glideslope to a decision altitude they are not precision approaches. The examiner does have the right based on the PTS to select the type of non-precision approaches. If the examiner request a pilot to demonstrate an RNAV approach and does not indicate which minimums, use LNAV or LNAV/VNAV minimums depending on the aircraft approval.

The examiner is required by the PTS to have the pilot fly one non-precision approach with reference to backup or "fail down" instrumentation or navigation display depending on the aircraft's avionics configuration. Be prepared and work with your instructor on the different possibilities based on the aircraft avionics configuration.

Don't forget about stabilized approach procedures. Remember the typical visual descent point (VDP) is a 3° approach path that intersects the MDA, if no obstacles are present. Look at the airport diagram ahead of time to determine if a VASI or PAPI is available and the descent angle. Determine a VDP before beginning the approach. If the pilot obtains visual reference with the runway past the VDP, it may require an excessive descent rate which is considered an unstabilized approach. If the pilot cannot conduct a stabilized approach to the runway, the pilot should execute a missed approach and try the approach again or select another approach.

SAFO09011

During a non-precision approach procedure, the descent from the final approach altitude to the minimum descent altitude (MDA) requires disciplined piloting technique and increased situational awareness to accommodate the pilot workload during this segment of the approach. As the complexity of the approach procedure increases, such as multiple step-down fixes or a circling approach, the pilot's workload increases. Environmental concerns such as night operations and weather conditions at minimums provide a cumulative effect on pilot workload. The workload under the aforementioned conditions increases significantly for single pilot operations. Therefore, operators should evaluate and, if necessary, implement appropriate procedures to reduce workload issues applicable to nonprecision approaches.

Such procedures should include the use of vertical navigation (VNAV) (if equipped) during nonprecision approaches, as a means to achieve a constant angle of descent approach profile from the final approach fix (FAF) to MDA. If the airplane is not VNAV equipped, the operator should develop procedures that address approach profile techniques using a stabilized constant angle of descent from the FAF to arrive at the published MDA prior to the published visual descent point (VDP). If the approach does not have a published VDP, the flightcrew may determine a point along the course between the FAF and Missed Approach Point (MAP) that would be appropriate for a VDP. With the runway environment in sight, and at the VDP or established on glidepath by means of a visual landing aid, the flightcrew may begin a normal descent from MDA to the landing runway. Objective 10 indicates the pilot should depart the MDA at a point where the descent to the runway is at a normal rate using normal maneuvering.

Operators should place a strong emphasis in their procedures relative to altitude management throughout the approach procedure. Particular attention should focus on methods and procedures established for use by the flight crew to manage their descent and maintain published altitudes along with appropriate descents from altitudes to either the next altitude or the landing runway, as appropriate.

Operators should focus on the use of thorough approach briefing content techniques to communicate to the crew how the approach will be flown. The operator's procedures should require the use of an operable autopilot, if installed, to reduce workload issues. Proper altitude management and awareness techniques are crucial in reducing landing accidents and should be incorporated into the operator's procedures. Equally important, the operator's procedures should require good crew communication and coordination techniques.

As stated earlier, single pilot operations have a much higher demand on the pilot. Therefore, careful consideration must be used in the development of single pilot constant angle of descent procedures. It is imperative that the operator's procedures focus on techniques for mitigating risk factors associated with single pilot nonprecision approach operations. The use of an autopilot during all instrument approaches should be required to reduce workloads.

Disconnect Between FAA Documents

Located in 8900.2 under section 10 is information about conducting an ATP certification, including additional category/class ratings at the ATP certification level. Located in this section is information to be used as guidance by the general aviation examiner and is as follows.

> "Additionally, although a lateral approach procedure with vertical guidance (LPV) is technically not considered a precision approach, it can be used as one of the precision approaches. The global positioning system (GPS) equipment must be instrument certified and contain the current database. Although LPV and lateral navigation (LNAV)/vertical navigation (VNAV) approaches are technically a nonprecision approaches, because of the availability of a glide path, they may not be used to demonstrate nonprecision approaches."

There is no restriction in the ATP PTS about not allowing a pilot to use VNAV during a non-precision RNAV approach. The FAA encourages the use of VNAV to promote stabilized approaches and increase safety.

8900.1 Volume 5 has a section Flight Test Events in Airplanes, ATP Applicants Engaged in Operations Under Title 14 CFR Part 121, 135, or 91 Subpart K. Under section B, Nonprecision Approaches, inspectors and examiners shall require applicants to demonstrate two nonprecision instrument approaches that are authorized in the operator's operations specifications. Inspectors and examiners shall allow the applicant to use any aid normally available in the cockpit, such as the flight director and drift and groundspeed readouts (operation specifications are used under Part 121 and 135).

SAFO 09011 is intended for part 121 and 135 operators but what is typically good for them is good for Part 91 pilots. The basic point in this safety alert is that pilots should use VNAV to the MDA if available. If VNAV is not available the operator/pilot should develop procedures that address approach profile techniques using a stabilized constant angle of descent from the FAF to arrive at the published MDA prior to the published visual descent point (VDP).

Let's take a look at a hypothetical situation. A pilot is taking the ATP practical test in an aircraft with approved VNAV capability. The FAA is clearly encouraging the use of VNAV during non-precision approach procedures (LNAV). What would you do if during the practical test the examiner said that you can not use VNAV on a non-precision approach (LNAV)? One option would be to ask the examiner why? There is no restriction in the PTS, POH/AFM or any of the references under the non-precision approach task. The only restriction is in 8900.2. There is plenty of encouragement by the FAA to use VNAV. Granted he can request a pilot to demonstrate a dive and drive type of approach, but the FAA is encouraging the use of VNAV or constant rate approaches for safety. The examiner really should follow the ATP PTS and allow the pilot to use all available equipment to operate and demonstrate the highest level of safety. A pilot using all available resources to demonstrate the highest level of safety also demonstrates excellent aeronautical decision making and that is to be evaluated during the practical test.

AIM

- It is FAA policy to design IAPs with minimum altitudes established at fixes/waypoints to achieve optimum stabilized (constant rate) descents within each procedure segment. This design can enhance the safety of the operations and contribute toward reduction in the occurrence of controlled flight into terrain (CFIT) accidents. Additionally, the National Transportation Safety Board (NTSB) recently emphasized that pilots could benefit from publication of the appropriate IAP descent angle for a stabilized descent on final approach. The RNAV IAP format includes the descent angle to the hundredth of a degree; e.g., 3.00 degrees. The angle will be provided in the graphically depicted descent profile.

- The stabilized approach may be performed by reference to vertical navigation information provided by WAAS or LNAV/VNAV systems; or for LNAV only systems, by the pilot determining the appropriate aircraft attitude/groundspeed combination to attain a constant rate descent which best emulates the published angle. To aid the pilot, U.S. Government Terminal Procedures Publication charts publish an expanded Rate of Descent Table on the inside of the back hard cover for use in planning and executing precision descents under known or approximate groundspeed conditions.

Can I use VNAV to LNAV only minimums?

AC20-138B

There may be occasions where it is operationally advantageous to use the LNAV line of minima rather than the LNAV/VNAV minima during an instrument approach procedure. It is acceptable for approved baro-VNAV installations to provide advisory vertical guidance when using the LNAV line of minima. **However, during these operations, the flight crew must use the primary barometric altimeter as the primary reference for compliance with all altitude restrictions associated with the instrument approach procedure; including compliance with all associated step-down fixes.**

Baro-VNAV is subject to temperature and pressure altitude (i.e., correct altimeter setting) performance limitations that could potentially cause advisory vertical path guidance to fall below step-down fixes on LNAV approaches.

Documents supporting VNAV use:

SAFO 09011

8900.2

AC20-138B

AC90-97

"Victory is the child of preparation
and determination."
–SEAN HAMPTON

TASK E: CIRCLING APPROACH

References

- Part 61- 61.157 areas of operation

- POH/AFM

- AIM

- Standard Instrument Approach Procedure Charts (SIAP)

- FAA-H-8261-1 - Instrument Procedures Handbook

- FAA-H-8083-15 - Instrument Flying Handbook

Applicant Note: Expect this task to be combined with other tasks to include Area VI, Task D.

Objective: To determine that the applicant:

1. Exhibits satisfactory knowledge of circling approach categories, speeds, and procedures to a specified runway.

2. In simulated or actual instrument conditions to MDA, accomplishes the circling approach selected by the examiner.

3. Demonstrates sound judgment and knowledge of the airplane maneuvering capabilities throughout the circling approach.

4. Confirms the direction of traffic and adheres to all restrictions and instructions issued by ATC.

5. Descends at a rate that ensures arrival at the MDA at, or prior to, a point from which a normal circle-to-land maneuver can be accomplished.

6. Avoids descent below the appropriate circling MDA or exceeding the visibility criteria until in a position from which a descent to a normal landing can be made.

7. Maneuvers the airplane, after reaching the authorized circling approach altitude, by visual references to maintain a flightpath that permits a normal landing on a runway that requires at

least a 90° change of direction, from the final approach course, to align the aircraft for landing.

8. Performs the procedure without excessive maneuvering and without exceeding the normal operating limits of the airplane (the angle of bank should not exceed 30°).

9. Maintains the desired altitude within −0, +100 feet, heading/track within ±5°, the airspeed/V-speed within ±5 knots, but not less than the airspeed as specified in the POH or the AFM.

10. Uses the appropriate airplane configuration for normal and abnormal situations and procedures.

11. Turns in the appropriate direction, when a missed approach is dictated during the circling approach, and uses the correct procedure and airplane configuration.

12. Performs all procedures required for the circling approach and airplane control in a smooth, positive, and timely manner.

Explained

Prior to beginning the approach calculate a VDP and/or determine what descent rate will be necessary to ensure that objective 5 is achieved. I see a lot of pilots that think there is a need to dive and drive to the MDA but this really is not necessary on most circling approaches. Determine what a comfortable, safe descent rate will arrive at the MDA prior to the point where the normal circle to land maneuver will begin.

I've seen a few pilots in the simulator arrive at the MDA and not add sufficient power to maintain at or above a safe maneuvering speed. Some pilots have become so focused on other tasks, the pilot forgets to add power and stalls. Every pilot should know exactly what power setting is required at the MDA to maintain the target airspeed in the selected configuration. I do mean a specific airspeed, not a range.

Missed Approach

The circling maneuver requires the pilot be thinking ahead. Objective 8 indicates a pilot is to perform the procedure without excessive maneuvering and the bank **should** not exceed 30°. Many pilots do overshoot the final approach path and have to maneuver back. If this happens, make sure to smoothly maneuver back to the final approach path and try not to exceed 30° of bank. If the aircraft is not in a position for a stabilized approach or excessive maneuvering will be required, execute a missed approach.

If during the circling approach a missed approach is required, some examiners might view this as a failure of the task, and some might see it as the pilot making a good decision and realizing the aircraft was out of position to make a safe landing. Objective 11 indicates that if a missed approach is necessary, the pilot turns in the appropriate direction. None of the objectives indicate the pilot must land the airplane and not execute a missed approach procedure.

I have spoken with examiners that indicated they would fail a pilot on the circling approach task if the pilot executed a missed approach due to not being in a good position to land the airplane. I realize if a pilot executes a missed approach and the maneuver was seriously in doubt then I can understand a failure. But if a pilot was not on the correct approach target profile and made a good decision that a missed approach was the safest maneuver, then what objective of the task can an examiner fail the pilot on? I don't see one. The real question comes down to was a maneuver seriously in doubt or just a little bit off and the pilot demonstrated good aeronautical decision making. On the second attempt the pilot really should be able to land the aircraft.

If below the MDA and a go around is necessary the AIM indicates "the aircraft is clear of obstacles when at or above the MDA while inside the circling area." Get above the MDA as soon as possible then climb within the protected circling area.

Always be prepared for a missed approach during any approach, but the circling approach requires a little thinking in advance. Review the AIM. After beginning the circling maneuver and then executing a missed approach, the AIM indicates to turn towards the airport. Think about this in advance and during the approach briefing include how the missed approach will be flown.

Bank Angle

Objective 8 indicates the pilot **should** not exceed a bank angle of 30°. The key word is should. Located in the beginning of 8900.1 the word **should** is defined as guidance. "Guidance information is information considered guiding in nature and will contain terms such as "should" or "may." These terms indicate actions that are desirable, permissive, or not mandatory, and allow flexibility." 4

If a pilot momentarily exceeds 30° of bank the pilot should immediately correct back to a bank angle less than 30°. As long as a maneuver was never seriously in doubt and the pilot did not consistently exceed this bank angle the pilot should not fail the task.

Altitude

Objective 9 requires a pilot to maintain the desired altitude within -0, +100 feet. Most pilots will be using the autopilot during this maneuver and if the MDA is set in the altitude selector, as the aircraft captures the selected altitude it may descend below the MDA while it captures the altitude selected. Be careful and decide how to handle this. One technique is add altitude to the MDA, for example 30 feet or more and select this altitude in the altitude selector. This will prevent the autopilot from momentarily descending below the MDA.

AIM: Descent below the MDA, including during the missed approach, is not authorized unless the visual conditions stated in 14 CFR Section 91.175 exist. 5-4-5

Plan Ahead:

- Target airspeed and power setting at the MDA.

- Is a higher altitude in the altitude selector for the MDA needed?

- Review missed approach procedures for a circling approach.

- To achieve landing performance as indicated in the POH what airspeed and altitude is required crossing the threshold?

- How are you going to perform a stabilized approach?

Most aircraft used for an ATP checkride will fit in the following categories:

- Category A, speed less than 91 knots and has a circling radius of 1.3 NM.

- Category B, speed 121 knots to less than 141 knots and has a circling radius of 1.5 NM.

- Category C, speed 141 knots to less than 166 knots and has a circling radius of 1.7 NM.

"Confidence is preparation. Everything
else is beyond your control."

–RICHARD KLINE

TASK F: MISSED APPROACH

References

- Part 61- 61.157 areas of operation

- POH/AFM

- AIM

- Standard Instrument Approach Procedure Charts (SIAP)

- FAA-H-8083-15 - Instrument Flying Handbook

- FAA-H-8261-1 - Instrument Procedures Handbook

Note: The applicant must perform two missed approaches with one being from a precision approach (ILS, MLS, or GLS). One complete published missed approach must be accomplished. Additionally, in multiengine airplanes, a missed approach must be accomplished with one engine inoperative (or simulated inoperative). The engine failure may be experienced anytime prior to the initiation of the approach, during the approach, or during the transition to the missed approach attitude and configuration.

Descending below the MDA or continuing a precision approach below DH/DA as appropriate, unless the runway environment is in sight is considered unsatisfactory performance. However, even if the missed approach is properly initiated at DA/DH, most airplanes descend below DA/DH because of the momentum of the airplane transitioning from a stabilized approach to a missed approach. This descent below DA/DH is not considered unsatisfactory, as long as the precision approach was not continued below DA/DH.

Objective: To determine that the applicant:

1. Exhibits satisfactory knowledge of missed approach procedures associated with standard instrument approaches to include reference to standby (backup or fail down) instruments.

2. Initiates the missed approach procedure promptly by the timely application of power, establishes the proper climb

attitude, and reduces drag in accordance with the approved procedures.

3. Reports to ATC, beginning the missed approach procedure.

4. Complies with the appropriate missed approach procedure or ATC clearance.

5. Advises ATC any time the applicant is unable to maneuver the airplane to comply with a clearance.

6. Follows the recommended airplane checklist items or coordinates with crew to ensure completion of checklist items in a timely manner and as recommended by the manufacturer appropriate to the go-around procedure for the airplane used.

7. Requests clearance, if appropriate, to the alternate airport, another approach, a holding fix, or as directed by the examiner.

8. Maintains the desired altitudes ±100 feet, airspeed ±5 knots, heading ±5°; and accurately tracks courses, radials, and bearings.

Explained

During the practical test a pilot will perform two missed approaches and one of them will be from a precision approach. One of the missed approaches will be a complete missed approach. If flying a multiengine airplane, one missed approach will have to be with one engine inoperative. Pay attention, the engine failure for this task can occur anytime prior to the approach, during the approach, or during the transition to the missed approach.

There are some basic procedures that need to be accomplished during a missed approach for every aircraft. These procedures need to be rehearsed, organized, and accomplished very smoothly. Here is a list of possibilities:

• Set the appropriate missed approach power setting as indicated in the POH.

- Establish the appropriate pitch attitude for the aircraft. Many aircraft have a go around setting for the flight director and the pilot should pitch to this. If the aircraft does not have a flight director, the pilot should have a specific pitch attitude to establish. There is no excuse for not knowing exactly what pitch attitude to establish. I see many pilots who just raise the nose of the aircraft with no target pitch.

- Appropriately reduce drag by retracting the landing gear and flaps as indicated in the POH.

- Set the appropriate navigation settings to establish the aircraft on the missed approach procedure.

- Notify ATC.

- Complete the appropriate checklist.

There may be something else a pilot would like to add to this list but this is a basic list that applies to any aircraft. If the practical test will be single pilot, rehearse this procedure and be able to accomplish the procedure very smoothly. If the practical test will be as a crew the missed approach procedure should be very coordinated between the two pilots and there should be no question about who does what.

During a missed approach procedure the main focus should be flying the aircraft. Break up the missed approach procedure into two sections, first fly the aircraft by establishing the appropriate power setting, pitch attitude and appropriate configuration change. After this is accomplished set the avionics to navigate the missed approach procedure.

During most missed approach procedures, I think each step can be done in the exact same order every time and be done very smoothly. Granted there are some missed approach procedures that may require modification, for example an immediate turn. Any modification should be briefed during the approach briefing so both pilots understand what to expect.

Once a single pilot or a crew has a well-established missed approach procedure, it is amazing how smooth they execute a missed approach.

The opposite where there is no order to the missed approach procedure, either single pilot or crew, it is often a disaster with a high chance of mistakes.

The examiner may test a pilots aeronautical decision-making in objective 7. Be prepared to follow through with the scenario and make a decision as PIC.

Checklist:

- Have a well-established missed approach profile and procedures?

- Be able to easily set up the avionics for missed approach procedure.

- What is the target pitch attitude and airspeed during the missed approach procedure?

- Does the copilot fully understand what is expected of him during the missed approach procedure? Do I understand what is expected of me?

- Does the POH offer any guidance and/or a checklist for missed approach procedure?

"By failing to prepare you are preparing to fail."

–BENJAMIN FANKLIN

VI. Landings and Approaches to Landings

Note: Notwithstanding the authorizations for the combining of maneuvers and for the waiver of maneuvers, the applicant must make at least three actual landings (one to a full stop). These landings must include the types listed in this Area of Operation; however, more than one type may be combined where appropriate (i.e., crosswind and landing from a precision approach or landing with simulated power-plant failure, etc.). For all landings, touchdown at the touchdown markings - 250' to +500' or where there are no runway aiming point markings, 750' to 1,500' from the approach threshold of the runway. Deceleration to taxi speed (20 knots or less on dry pavement, 10 knots or less on contaminated pavement) should be demonstrated on at least one landing to within the calculated landing distance plus 25% for the actual conditions with the runway centerline between the main landing gear. At no time will the outcome of the rollout and subsequent taxi be in doubt. Go-arounds will incur no penalty if successful. "Successful" is defined as no surface contact except for the landing gear on the runway. An amphibian type rating must bear the limitation "Limited to Land" or "Limited to Sea," as appropriate, unless the applicant demonstrates proficiency in both land and sea operations.

TASK A: NORMAL AND CROSSWIND APPROACHES AND LANDINGS

References

- Part 61- 61.157 areas of operation

- POH/AFM

- FAA-H-8083-3 - Airplane Flying Handbook

Note: In an airplane with a single powerplant, unless the applicant holds a commercial pilot certificate, he or she must accomplish three accuracy approaches and spot landings from an altitude of 1,000 feet or less, with the engine power lever in idle and 180° of change in direction. The airplane must touch the ground in a normal landing attitude beyond and within 200 feet of a designated line or point on the runway. At least one landing must be from a forward slip.

Objective: To determine that the applicant:

1. Exhibits satisfactory knowledge of normal and crosswind approaches and landings including recommended approach angles, airspeeds, V-speeds, configurations, performance limitations, wake turbulence, LAHSO, and safety factors (as appropriate to the airplane).

2. Establishes the approach and landing configuration appropriate for the runway and meteorological conditions, and adjusts the powerplant controls as required.

3. Maintains a ground track that ensures the desired traffic pattern will be flown, taking into account any obstructions and ATC or examiner instructions.

4. Verifies existing wind conditions, makes proper correction for drift, and maintains a precise ground track.

5. Maintains a stabilized approach and the desired airspeed/V-speed within ±5 knots.

6. Accomplishes a smooth, positively controlled transition from final approach to touchdown.

7. Maintains positive directional control and crosswind correction during the after-landing roll.

8. Uses spoilers, prop reverse, thrust reverse, wheel brakes, and other drag/braking devices, as appropriate, in such a manner to bring the airplane to a safe stop.

9. Completes the applicable after-landing checklist items or coordinates with crew to ensure completion of checklist items in a timely manner and as recommended by the manufacturer.

Explained

For all landings, touchdown should be 500 to 3000 feet past the runway threshold, not to exceed one-third of the runway length, with the runway centerline between the main landing gear. Pilots sometimes have trouble accomplishing this performance due to unstabilized approaches, improper airspeed control, poor crosswind technique and control. Pilots should work with their instructor to make sure that this performance is not a problem.

Let's use an example of a pilot landing from an approach and the pilot touched down 4,000 feet past the runway threshold. Should that pilot fail the practical test? I would like to point out under this area of operation the word <u>should</u> is being used. Refer to the task Circling Approach where I explained the word should is not restrictive.

If a pilot is landing too far down the runway the pilot is probably not maintaining a stabilized approach and the desired airspeed on final. Objective 5 indicates the pilot is to maintain a stabilized approach and the desired airspeed/V-speed within +/-5 knots. Even though the pilot should touchdown 500 to 3000 feet past the runway threshold, the examiner would most likely fail the pilot for not maintaining a stabilized approach and the appropriate airspeed on final approach to landing.

If the speeds and profiles in the POH are flown, there is no reason the aircraft should not easily meet the ATP PTS requirements.

The pilot should also understand the landing performance section of the POH. The POH will identify the associated conditions that will achieve the landing distance indicated in the POH. If the pilot is not operating the aircraft as indicated by the POH there's always a greater chance of a runway overrun. If the approach to landing and landing were borderline, the examiner may question the pilot to determine if the pilot exhibits satisfactory knowledge of normal and crosswind approaches and landings including recommended approach angles, airspeeds, V-speeds, configurations, performance limitations as indicated in objective 1 of this task. This knowledge verification can occur in the aircraft or after the flight.

Example, the pilot touched down 4,000 feet past the runway threshold due to an unstabilized approach. Let's say the runway was 10,000 feet long and even touching down 4000 feet down the runway in certain aircraft will still leave plenty of runway available. When questioned by the examiner the pilot may respond "there was 10,000 feet of runway and a little extra float wouldn't affect anything." Like I indicated the PTS indicates the landing <u>should</u> be 500 to 3000 feet past the runway threshold. I think the examiner could easily fail the pilot under objective 1 for not demonstrating satisfactory knowledge of landing procedures and recommended airspeeds and also objective 5, not maintaining the appropriate airspeed.

Study the performance section of your POH/AFM. The POH/AFM explains exactly what is required to achieve the landing performance as indicated in the POH. For example in the King Air 350 POH, in the beginning of the performance section it is stated that the pilot is to maintain the Vref crossing the threshold, on a 3° approach path, at 50 feet over the threshold reduce the power to idle. It is that simple and can easily be achieved. Vref is approximately 1.3 x Vso and is a safe margin above stalling speed. In the King Air and other aircraft, pilots tend to cross the threshold at an airspeed above Vref.

An instructor was working with a pilot in the King Air who demonstrated a very unstabilized approach. The weather was at category 1 ILS minimums and when he obtained visual on the approach lights and runway, he extended the flaps to the landing position, the aircraft ballooned, the airspeed was fast, and he floated down the runway to a point he had to make a go around. If this was a practical test he would of failed. He flew another ILS stabilized in the landing configuration at Vref and he easily made a normal landing within the touchdown zone.

Why do pilots feel they need to maintain a speed above Vref on final approach and crossing the threshold? Some instructors believe one reason is a lack of knowledge and understanding of aircraft performance. There is absolutely no reason to be 10 to 20 knots above Vref except if a windshear factor is being applied. Not to mention it is an unstabilized approach. Additional airspeed requires additional landing distance, increased floating and therefore a increased runway overrun possibility. Work with your instructor, study stabilized approaches, read the POH and increase your knowledge of aircraft performance if necessary. Not to mention according to objective 1, the examiner can ask questions on performance if the pilot is not demonstrating satisfactory knowledge.

For example, a pilot taking a practical test crosses the threshold Vref +15. What would you do as an examiner if a pilot did this? At a minimum the examiner should ask questions to verify knowledge of aircraft performance.

Completes Checklist

I would like to point out that every task under the area of operation landings and approaches to landings requires the pilot to complete the applicable after landing checklist items. Even though a pilot may be taxiing for another takeoff, to cover all of the objectives complete the after landing, and then do the before takeoff checklist.

Checklist:

- Do I understand the performance section of the POH?

- Do I understand what a stabilized approach is?

- On landing do I always touchdown 500 feet to 3000 feet down the runway or the first one third of the runway?

- Do I always touchdown with the runway centerline between the main wheels?

- Do I normally complete all appropriate checklists?

"If the people knew how hard I had to work to gain my mastery, it wouldn't seem wonderful at all."

—MICHELANGELO

TASK B: LANDING FROM A PRECISION APPROACH

References

- Part 61- 61.157 areas of operation

- POH/AFM

- FAA-H-8083-15 -Instrument Flying Handbook

Note: If circumstances beyond the control of the applicant prevent an actual landing, the examiner may accept an approach to a point where, in his or her judgment, a safe landing and a full stop could have been made, and credit given for a missed approach. Where a simulator approved for landing from a precision approach is used, the approach may be continued through the landing and credit given for one of the landings required by this AREA OF OPERATION.

Applicant Note: Expect other tasks to be combined with this task (to include Area VI, Task C for multiengine airplanes).

Objective: To determine that the applicant:

1. Exhibits awareness of landing in sequence from a precision approach.

2. Considers factors to be applied to the approach and landing such as displaced thresholds, meteorological conditions, NOTAMs, and ATC or examiner instructions.

3. Uses the airplane configuration and airspeed/V-speeds, as appropriate.

4. Maintains, during the final approach segment, glide slope and localizer indications within applicable standards of deviation, and the recommended airspeed/V-speed ±5 knots.

5. Applies gust/wind factors as recommended by the manufacturer, and takes into account meteorological phenomena such as wind shear, microburst, and other related safety of flight factors.

6. Accomplishes the appropriate checklist items or coordinates with crew to ensure timely completion of checklist items in a timely manner and as recommended by the manufacturer or approved method.

7. Transitions smoothly from simulated instrument meteorological conditions (IMC) at a point designated by the examiner, maintaining positive airplane control.

8. Accomplishes a smooth, positively controlled transition from final approach to touchdown.

9. Maintains positive directional control and crosswind correction during the after-landing roll.

10. Uses spoilers, prop reverse, thrust reverse, wheel brakes, and other drag/braking devices, as appropriate, in such a manner to bring the airplane to a safe stop after landing.

11. Accomplishes the appropriate after-landing checklist items or coordinates with crew to ensure completion of after-landing checklist items in a timely manner and as recommended by the manufacturer.

"If I had eight hours to chop down a tree,
I'd spend six sharpening my axe."
–ABRAHAM LINCOLN

TASK C: APPROACH AND LANDING WITH (SIMULATED) POWERPLANT FAILURE - MULTIENGINE AIRPLANE

References

- Part 61- 61.157 areas of operation

- POH/AFM

- FAA-H-8083-3 - Airplane Flying Handbook

Note: In airplanes with three powerplants, the applicant must follow a procedure (if approved) that approximates the loss of two powerplants, the center and one outboard powerplant. In other multiengine airplanes, the applicant must follow a procedure, which simulates the loss of 50 percent of available powerplants, the loss being simulated on one side of the airplane.

Applicant Note: Expect task to be combined with other tasks (to include Area V, Task E). May be limited by aircraft parameters under ambient conditions at examiner's discretion.

Objective: To determine that the applicant:

1. Exhibits satisfactory knowledge of the flight characteristics and controllability associated with maneuvering to a landing with powerplant(s) inoperative (or simulated inoperative) including the controllability factors associated with maneuvering, and the applicable emergency procedures.

2. Maintains positive airplane control. Establishes a bank of approximately 5°, if required, or as recommended by the manufacturer, to maintain coordinated flight, and properly trims for that condition.

3. Sets powerplant controls, reduces drag as necessary, correctly identifies and verifies the inoperative powerplant(s) after the failure (or simulated failure).

4. Maintains the operating powerplant(s) within acceptable operating limits.

5. Follows the prescribed airplane checklist or coordinates with crew to ensure timely completion of checklist items in a timely manner and as recommended by the manufacturer, and verifies the procedures for securing the inoperative powerplant(s).

6. Proceeds toward the nearest suitable airport.

7. Maintains, prior to beginning the final approach segment, the desired altitude ±100 feet, the desired airspeed ±10 knots, the desired heading ±5°; and accurately tracks courses, radials, and bearings.

8. Establishes the approach and landing configuration appropriate for the runway or landing area, and meteorological conditions; and adjusts the powerplant controls as required.

9. Maintains a stabilized approach and the desired airspeed/ V-speed within ±5 knots.

10. Accomplishes a smooth, positively controlled transition from final approach to touchdown.

11. Maintains positive directional control and crosswind corrections during the after-landing roll.

12. Uses spoilers, prop reverse, thrust reversers, wheel brakes, and other drag/braking devices, as appropriate, in such a manner to bring the airplane to a safe stop after landing.

13. Accomplishes the appropriate after-landing checklist items or coordinates with crew to ensure completion of after-landing checklist items in a timely manner and as recommended by the manufacturer.

Explained

Pilots should have a very specific target airspeed and power setting for single engine level flight. Often the POH will not provide a profile for single engine operations. Having profiles will reduce the pilots workload and prevent losing too much airspeed during an engine failure.

Have a specific target airspeed and power setting for the 3° approach path. The POH probably gives a specific airspeed to maintain, know exactly what power setting will maintain that airspeed.

For example, if the single engine approach and landing checklist states maintain Vref +15 with an approach flap setting while descending for landing, then according to objective 9, maintain that airspeed ± 5 knots. Again this is one of those areas I've noticed pilots feeling the need to maintain a higher airspeed.

The best performance is always by the pilots that has very specific targets when it comes to power settings and airspeeds.

"I run on the road, long before I
dance under the lights."

–MUHAMMAD ALI

TASK D: LANDING FROM A CIRCLING APPROACH

References

- Part 61- 61.157 areas of operation

- POH/AFM

- AIM

- FAA-H-8083-15 - Instrument Flying Handbook

Applicant Note: Expect task to be combined with other tasks (to include previous task, Task C for multiengine aircraft.)

Objective: To determine that the applicant:

1. Exhibits knowledge of a landing from a circling approach.

2. Selects, and complies with, a circling approach procedure to a specified runway.

3. Considers the environmental, operational, and meteorological factors, which affect a landing from a circling approach.

4. Confirms the direction of traffic and adheres to all restrictions and instructions issued by ATC.

5. Descends at a rate that ensures arrival at the MDA at, or prior to, a point from which a normal circle-to-land maneuver can be accomplished.

6. Avoids descent below the appropriate circling MDA or exceeding the visibility criteria until in a position from which a descent to a normal landing can be made.

7. Accomplishes the appropriate checklist items or coordinates with crew to ensure completion of checklist items in a timely manner and as recommended by the manufacturer or approved method.

8. Maneuvers the airplane, after reaching the authorized circling approach altitude, by visual references, to maintain a flight

path that requires at least a 90° change of direction, from the final approach course, to align the aircraft for landing.

9. Performs the maneuver without excessive maneuvering and without exceeding the normal operating limits of the airplane. The angle of bank should not exceed 30°.

10. Maintains the desired altitude within +100, −0 feet, heading within ±5°, and approach airspeed/V-speed within ±5 knots.

11. Uses the appropriate airplane configuration for normal and abnormal situations and procedures.

12. Performs all procedures required for the circling approach and airplane control in a timely, smooth, and positive manner.

13. Accomplishes a smooth, positively controlled transition to final approach and touchdown or to a point where in the opinion of the examiner that a safe full stop landing could be made.

14. Maintains positive directional control and crosswind correction during the after landing roll.

15. Uses spoilers, prop reverse, thrust reverse, wheel brakes, and other drag/braking devices, as appropriate, in such a manner to bring the airplane to a safe stop.

16. Accomplishes the appropriate after-landing checklist items or coordinates with crew to ensure completion of after-landing checklist items in a timely manner and as recommended by the manufacturer, after clearing the runway in a timely manner and as recommended by the manufacturer.

Explained

Just like the task for a circling approach, the PTS indicates in objective 9 the bank angle should not exceed 30°. Again the FAA uses the word <u>should</u> which is not restrictive. If a pilot happens to exceed the 30° bank but promptly returns to a bank angle less than 30° and is not consistently exceeding 30°, the pilot will probably still pass the task. Another evaluation factor is to ask was the maneuver ever seriously in doubt? A pilot can briefly bank more than 30° and the maneuver not be in doubt.

"The most prepared are the most dedicated."
-RAYMOND BERRY

TASK H: REJECTED LANDING

References

- Part 61- 61.157 areas of operation

- POH/AFM

- AIM

- FSB Report

- FAA-H-8083-3 - Airplane Flying Handbook

Note: The maneuver may be combined with instrument, circling, or missed approach procedures, but instrument conditions need not be simulated below 100 feet above the runway. This maneuver should be initiated approximately 50 feet above the runway or landing area and approximately over the runway threshold or as recommended by the FSB Report.

For those applicants seeking a VFR only type rating in an airplane not capable of instrument flight, and where this maneuver is accomplished with a simulated engine failure, it should not be initiated at speeds or altitudes below that recommended in the POH.

Objective: To determine that the applicant:

1. Exhibits satisfactory knowledge of a rejected landing procedure including the conditions that dictate a rejected landing, the importance of a timely decision, LAHSO considerations, the recommended airspeed/V-speeds, and also the applicable "clean-up" procedure.

2. Makes a timely decision to reject the landing for actual or simulated circumstances and makes appropriate notification when safety-of-flight is not an issue.

3. Applies the appropriate power setting for the flight condition and establishes a pitch attitude necessary to obtain the desired performance.

4. Retracts the wing flaps/drag devices and landing gear, if appropriate, in the correct sequence and at a safe altitude, establishes a positive rate of climb and the appropriate airspeed/V-speed within ±5 knots.

5. Trims the airplane as necessary, and maintains the proper ground track during the rejected landing procedure.

6. Accomplishes the appropriate after-landing checklist items or coordinates with crew to ensure timely completion of checklist items, in accordance with approved procedures.

7. Reports reject to ATC in a timely manner, after executing reject procedures.

Explained

During this maneuver don't get in a hurry. Fly the airplane first, get the climb established and clean up the airplane as directed by the POH/AFM. Correctly navigate the aircraft. This is a maneuver that if chair flown enough, a pilot will have no problem executing it very smoothly with no mistakes. Even rehearsing in your mind will greatly improve performance.

> "You can't push anyone up the ladder
> unless he is ready to climb himself."
> **–ANDREW CARNEGIE**

TASK I: LANDING FROM A NO FLAP OR A NONSTANDARD FLAP APPROACH

References

- Part 61- 61.157 areas of operation

- POH/AFM

- FSB Report

- FAA-H-8083-3 - Airplane Flying Handbook

Note: This maneuver need not be accomplished for a particular airplane type if the Administrator has determined that the probability of flap extension failure on that type airplane is extremely remote due to system design. The examiner must determine whether checking on slats only and partial-flap approaches are necessary for the practical test. However, probability of asymmetrical flap failures should be considered in this making this determination.

Objective: To determine that the applicant:

1. Exhibits knowledge of the factors, which affect the flight characteristics of an airplane when full or partial flaps, leading edge flaps, and other similar devices become inoperative.

2. Uses the correct airspeeds/V-speeds for the approach and landing.

3. Maintains the proper airplane pitch attitude and flight path for the configuration, gross weight, surface winds, and other applicable operational considerations.

4. Uses runway of sufficient length for the zero or nonstandard flap condition.

5. Maneuvers the airplane to a point where a touchdown at an acceptable point on the runway and a safe landing to a full stop could be made.

6.   After landing, uses spoilers, prop reverse, thrust reverse, wheel brakes, and other drag/braking devices, as appropriate, in such a manner to bring the airplane to a safe stop.

Explained

Always set the speed bug to the appropriate Vref for a no flap or a nonstandard approach and landing. After completing the flaps up landing checklist, I have seen many pilots not reset the speed bug to the new Vref speed and leave the speed bug at the full flap Vref speed. If a pilot does this, there is a greater chance of slowing down to full flap Vref speed by mistake. Always follow the checklist and set the correct Vref speed. This mistake will cause a failure of the task.

Often determining the landing distance required for a no flap or nonstandard flap landing is not easily accessible. It may require the pilot to access the POH/AFM to determine the landing distance required. One technique, is to determine under worst-case conditions for temperature, altitude and weight for the practical test and write that in the checklist. For example, if my practical test was conducted at KCLT, I would determine ahead of time what runway length would be required at the hottest temperature that day and maximum gross weight. I would then pencil this into the checklist for a nonstandard flap landing. This can also apply to normal day-to-day operations if a pilot tends to operate in a certain region.

Remember that prop reverse and thrust reversers are most effective at higher ground speeds. Use them to assist in stopping during a no flap landing.

"To be prepared against surprise
is to be trained. To be prepared for
surprise is to be educated."
–JAMES CARSE

VII. Normal and Abnormal Procedures

TASK A: NORMAL AND ABNORMAL PROCEDURES

References

- Part 61- 61.157 areas of operation

- POH/AFM

- FSB Report

Objective: To determine that the applicant:

1. Exhibits satisfactory knowledge of the normal and abnormal procedures of the systems, subsystems, and devices relative to the airplane type (as may be determined by the examiner); knows immediate action items to accomplish, if appropriate, and proper checklist to accomplish or to call for, if appropriate.

2. Demonstrates the proper use of the airplane systems, subsystems, and devices (as may be determined by the examiner) appropriate to the airplane, such as -

   a. powerplant.

   b. fuel system.

   c. electrical system.

   d. hydraulic system.

   e. environmental and pressurization systems.

   f. fire detection and extinguishing systems.

   g. navigation and avionics systems to include backup (fail down) modes and procedures.

   h. automatic flight control system, electronic flight instrument system, and related subsystems to include backup (fail down) modes and procedures.

   i. flight control systems.

j. anti-ice and deice systems.

k. airplane and personal emergency equipment.

l. other systems, subsystems, and devices specific to the type airplane, including make, model, and series.

Explained

The reference list is very short and the normal and abnormal procedures are obtained from the POH/AFM.

For a pilot to be thoroughly familiar with all emergency, abnormal and normal checklists it will take many hours of preparation. Skimming through checklists and lightly reading them will accomplish very little. From what I've observed, it takes studying the POH checklist sections many times to understand all aspects. For example ask yourself, when activating a certain switch in a checklist, what happens. A pilot ready for their practical test will be able to answer this question in every checklist for each item. Begin now and allow ample time to thoroughly review all checklists. I've seen many mistakes because a pilot did not understand the checklist completely. These mistakes can cause a practical test failure. During training pilots should ask the instructor to cover as many checklists as possible. In the simulator environment this is very easy to do.

From what I've observed in the simulator training environment, the average pilot is minimally knowledgeable about most checklists for a particular aircraft. Granted some of the checklist are not difficult and are easy to understand. But typically, during initial training and recurrent training it is not hard to find a few checklists the pilot really does not understand. It just comes down to putting the time into trying to understand each individual checklist.

Being able to locate the correct checklist in a timely manner is very important. It does state under the knowledge portion of objective 1 that the pilot should know what appropriate checklist to accomplish or call for. If a pilot is lost in determining what checklist to accomplish, that pilot has a chance of failing this task. The only way to ensure this does not happen is to be thoroughly familiar with all checklists.

Example. The examiner simulates a failure or in the simulator activates the actual failure of a system. The pilot does not know what checklist to use or incorrectly applies the appropriate checklist. The pilot failed to meet objective 1 and the task is failed.

Note the title of the task, this applies for normal procedures also.

No Procedure

What if an examiner gives the pilot a system failure that does not have a procedure or checklist in the POH? This may be considered not a good choice by the examiner because as long as the pilot improvises and gets the aircraft on the ground safely, that is it. For example, most aircraft that have an integrated avionics processor system (IAPS) do not have a checklist for an IAPS failure and this is a possible failure in many simulators. As long as the maneuver is never in doubt, the pilot should pass the task. I prefer to select failures that have a procedure in the POH to make the evaluation easier.

"When you're prepared, you're more confident. When you have a strategy, you're more comfortable."

–FRED COUPLES

VIII. Emergency Procedures

TASK A: EMERGENCY PROCEDURES

References

- Part 61- 61.157 areas of operation

- POH/AFM

Objective: To determine that the applicant:

1. Exhibits satisfactory knowledge of the emergency procedures (as may be determined by the examiner) relating to the particular airplane type.

2. Demonstrates the proper emergency procedures (as must be determined by the examiner) relating to the particular airplane type, such as -

   a. emergency descent (maximum rate).

   b. inflight fire and smoke removal.

   c. rapid decompression.

   d. emergency evacuation.

   e. airframe icing.

   f. others (as may be required by the AFM).

3. Demonstrates the proper procedure for any other emergency outlined (as determined by the examiner) in the appropriate approved AFM to include demonstration of flight by reference to standby flight instruments.

Explained

Everything that was stated in the previous task for normal and abnormal procedures applies to emergency procedures. Pilots must have certain portions of emergency procedures memorized as indicated by the POH/AFM. In most cases it is acceptable to not have the memory checklist items verbatim, but they should be done accurately and in the correct sequence.

8900.1, Volume 5, Chapter 1 deals with airmen certification for Parts 121/135 and general aviation. Under section 5-56 Oral Test Phase for Parts 121 and 135 is the best explanation of what is expected of the pilot with reference to emergency procedures and abnormal procedures. Under general aviation there is not a section that explains it in this manner, but what is good for 121/135 is good for part 91 pilots. Even under 8900.2 it is not explained in this manner like it is for part 121 or 135. This is one of the many examples of a disconnect between documents and organizations in the FAA. There should be one standard. I'm going to include this because I think it is a good example of how it should be, and it provides information for a good argument if you find yourself in a discussion of what is expected of you when it comes to memory sections of emergency procedures in the POH. [4, 5]

The following is the information is located in 8900.1.

"Applicants are expected to possess a broad understanding of the aircraft and its systems rather than a highly detailed knowledge of component design and construction. They should be able to demonstrate an understanding of the essential features of system design and how various systems interrelate. Applicants must be able to demonstrate such knowledge by interpreting cockpit indications and describing the condition of aircraft systems from these indications. Applicants are not expected to have memorized specific facts that are immediately available in reference manuals and checklists that are required to be in the cockpit. Applicants must, however, be able to state memory items on emergency checklists (in the correct sequence) and flight manual limitations from memory.

When a limitation is presented in terms of a gauge marking, the applicant should be able to state the operational significance of the marking but does not need to have memorized the appropriate value the marking represents. When a limitation is not clearly presented by such a marking, the applicant must be able to state the appropriate value from memory."

I think this explains what is expected clearly and should apply to all practical tests.

The examiner gets to select which emergency procedures the pilot will be required to demonstrate. This means pilots must be prepared for all emergency procedures. Begin early and set a goal to understand every emergency, normal and abnormal checklist in the POH/AFM.

Standby Instruments

Read objective 3. When I break down objective 3, I get the impression that the applicant must demonstrate flight by reference to standby flight instruments in order to complete the objective. In any case, be prepared for emergencies that would meet this objective.

"The secret of success in life is for a man to
be ready for his opportunity when it comes."
–BENJAMIN DISRAELI

IX. Postflight Procedures

TASK A: AFTER-LANDING PROCEDURES

References

- POH/AFM

Objective: To determine that the applicant:

1. Exhibits knowledge of safe after-landing, taxi, ramping, anchoring, docking, and mooring procedures, as appropriate.

2. Exhibits procedures to ensure the pilot maintains strict focus on the movement of the aircraft and ATC communications.

3. Demonstrates proficiency by maintaining correct and positive control. In airplanes equipped with float devices, this includes water taxiing, approaching a buoy, sailing, and docking.

4. Utilizes procedures for holding the pilot's workload to a minimum during taxi operations.

5. Maintains proper spacing on other aircraft, obstructions, and persons.

6. Utilizes taxi operation planning procedures, such as recording taxi instructions, reading back taxi clearances, and reviewing taxi routes on the airport diagram.

7. Utilizes procedures to ensure that clearance or instructions that are actually received are adhered to rather than the ones expected to be received.

8. Demonstrates procedures for briefing if a landing rollout to a taxiway exit will place the pilot in close proximity to another runway which can result in a runway incursion.

9. Accomplishes the applicable checklist items or coordinates with crew to ensure completion of checklist items in a timely manner and as recommended by the manufacturer and performs the recommended procedures.

10. Conducts appropriate after-landing/taxi procedures in the event the aircraft is on a taxiway that is between parallel runways.

11. Demonstrates specific procedures for operations at an airport with an operating air traffic control tower, with emphasis on ATC communications and runway entry/crossing authorizations.

12. Demonstrates and explains ATC communications and pilot actions before landing, and after landing at airports.

13. Maintains the desired track and speed.

14. Complies with instructions issued by ATC (or the examiner simulating ATC).

15. Observes runway hold lines, localizer and glide slope critical areas, and other surface control markings and lighting to prevent a runway incursion.

16. Maintains constant vigilance and airplane control during the taxi operation.

17. Demonstrates and/or explains procedural differences for night operations.

18. Demonstrates and explains the use(s) of aircraft exterior lighting and differences for day and night operations.

19. Explains and discusses the hazards of low visibility operations.

Explained

To ensure the highest level of safety and accuracy during single pilot operations the after landing procedures should be done with the aircraft stopped, with the parking brake set. If operating in a crew environment, it may be acceptable for the PF to continue taxiing while the PM completes the after landing checklist. If at a busy airport, as a single pilot it may be more practical to develop a flow for the after landing which will be verified complete by the checklist at a safe time with the aircraft stopped.

During low visibility conditions, the aircraft should be stopped while conducting a checklist. This is so both pilots can be heads up during taxi. Objective 2 is very clear that the pilot maintain strict focus on the movement of the aircraft and ATC communications. Objective 4 is also clear in that the pilot uses procedures for holding the pilot's workload to a minimum during taxi operations.

Imagine this situation, a pilot is operating an aircraft single pilot, after clearing the runway the pilot continues to taxi while accomplishing the after landing checklist in a read and do method. When the pilot is looking at the checklist there really is no pilot actively taxiing the airplane and looking outside. Objective 2 requires the pilot to maintain strict focus on the movement of the aircraft. Anytime the pilot is looking at a checklist, this is questionable. Some examiners may not disagree with a pilot who completes the after landing checklist by looking at the checklist and continuing taxiing, but I guarantee there are some examiners that will disagree and will not think it is safe. Even if a pilot thinks taxiing and completing a checklist by reading and doing is safe, error on the conservative side. Stop the aircraft, set the parking brake, complete the after landing checklist and then begin taxiing to the ramp. Or do a flow checklist and verify it was completed correctly when the aircraft is stopped.

Think about this example. The pilot is taxiing single pilot. The pilot looks at the after landing checklist and the aircraft obviously deviates from the centerline due to the pilot looking at the checklist. Even if it was a small deviation and the pilot looked up and corrected before it was ever a problem, did the pilot meet all of the objectives? The examiner may consider objectives 2, 4, 13, or 16 not achieved.

The following references are not part of the reference list of this task but do provide good guidance for this task. The only reference the examiner should use on this task is the POH/AFM. Example, the King Air 350 POH does not provide guidance for after landing flight crew procedures other than a checklist. The POH does not provide guidance for CRM or low visibility taxi operations. As long as the maneuver was never in doubt, compliance with the objectives and good decision making was demonstrated, the task is completed.

Example. The examiner has an after landing technique he thinks is very important. That technique is not in the reference list. The pilot met all of the objectives by maintaining very good control of the aircraft during taxi. The pilot demonstrated good situation awareness during the taxi. With reference to the practical test, that technique means nothing and the pilot cannot be evaluated on that item.

According to the PHAK

To give full attention to controlling the airplane during the landing roll, the after-landing check should be performed only after the airplane is brought to a complete stop clear of the active runway. There have been many cases of the pilot mistakenly grasping the wrong handle and retracting the landing gear, instead of the flaps, due to improper division of attention while the airplane was moving. However, this procedure may be modified if the manufacturer recommends that specific after-landing items be accomplished during landing rollout. For example, when performing a short-field landing, the manufacturer may recommend retracting the flaps on rollout to improve braking. In this situation, the pilot should make a positive identification of the flap control and retract the flaps.

AC91-73A

After landing and exiting the runway, nonessential communications and nonessential pilot actions should not be initiated until clear (on the inbound [terminal] side) of all runways.

Pilots should plan the timing and execution of aircraft checklists and company communications at the appropriate times. When planning these tasks, they should also consider the anticipated duration of the taxi operation, the locations of complex intersections and runway crossings, and the visibility along the taxi route. If possible during low visibility operations, pilots should conduct pre-departure checklists only when the aircraft is stopped or while taxiing straight ahead on a taxiway without complex intersections.

Night

The PTS now includes objectives under the tasks Taxiing and After Landing Procedures that includes night operations. Be prepared to answer questions on these objectives if the practical test is conducted during the day. Notice there is no exception to the objectives, the examiner must cover them.

"It's better to look ahead and prepare than to look back and regret."

–JACKIE JOYNER KERSEE

TASK F: PARKING AND SECURING

References

- POH/AFM

Objective: To determine that the applicant:

1. Demonstrates knowledge of the parking, and the securing airplane procedures.

2. Demonstrates knowledge of the airplane forms/logs to record the flight time/discrepancies.

3. Demonstrates knowledge of any installed and auxiliary aircraft security equipment, as appropriate.

Explained

According to the PHAK

Unless parking in a designated, supervised area, the pilot should select a location and heading which will prevent the propeller or jet blast of other airplanes from striking the airplane broadside. Whenever possible, the airplane should be parked headed into the existing or forecast wind. After stopping on the desired heading, the airplane should be allowed to roll straight ahead enough to straighten the nosewheel or tailwheel.

Engine Shutdown Check

Finally, the pilot should always use the procedures in the manufacturer's checklist for shutting down the engine and securing the airplane. The only reference for this task is the POH/AFM. If a pilot follows the appropriate checklist and any other guidance in the POH/AFM the task should be completed satisfactorily.

"If you are prepared, you will be confident, and will do the job."
–TOM LANDRY

Summary

With proper preparation for the ATP Practical Test a pilot can be completely prepared and understand exactly what is expected. Understanding what is expected of you can actually reduce your study time and stress. There is so much information available to pilots but the PTS does indicate what information is to be used during the practical test.

Now that you have read this book I think you have a much better understanding of the PTS and what is expected of you. I hope you feel much better about your preparation and chance of success.

References

1. Airbus Safety Library

2. AIM

3. Airline Transport Pilot and Aircraft Type Rating Practical Test Standards for Airplane.

4. Flight Standards Information Management System 8900.1

5. General Aviation Airman Designee Handbook 8900.2